Mysteries of the Bible

MYSTERIES OF THE BIBLE

MYSTERIES OF THE BIBLE

FROM THE LOCATION OF EDEN TO THE SHROUD OF TURIN

A COLLECTION OF ESSAYS PUBLISHED
BY
THE BIBLICAL ARCHAEOLOGY SOCIETY

Contributors:

Emmanuel Anati

Israel Finkelstein

Rivka Gonen

Howard W. Goodkind

Hillel Halkin

Ronald S. Hendel

Ephraim Isaac

Allen Kerkeslager

Simo Parpola

Bezalel Porten

James Sauer

Hershel Shanks

Suzanne F. Singer

William Stiebing

Robert A. Wild

Ben Witherington III

Edited by Molly Dewsnap Meinhardt

Biblical Archaeology Society
Washington, D.C.

All essays previously appeared in *Biblical Archaeology Review* or *Bible Review*.
Design by Scribe.

Library of Congress Cataloging-in-Publication Data

Mysteries of the Bible : from the location of Eden to the Shroud of
Turin : a collection of essays published by the Biblical Archaeology
Society / edited by Molly Dewsnap Meinhardt ;
contributors, Emmanuel Anati ... [et al.].
    p. cm.
  Includes bibliographical references.
  ISBN 1-880317-73-7
  1. Bible--Miscellanea. 2. Bible--Antiquities--Miscellanea.
  I. Meinhardt, Molly Dewsnap. II. Anati, Emmanuel.

BS615.M98 2004
220.9'3--dc22

                              2004014022

Table of Contents

Introduction

"Is it true," a caller asks, "that the wheels of Pharaoh's chariot have been found in the Red Sea?" "Have U.S. satellite photos revealed the remains of Noah's Ark, preserved intact in ice, on Mt. Ararat?" "Is the Ark of the Covenant hidden beneath the Temple Mount in Jerusalem?"

The callers who reach the editorial offices of the Biblical Archaeology Society are excited and hopeful; their questions intriguing. But the answers they receive (in this case, no, no and there's no evidence of this) are often—though not always—disappointing.

In many ways, their questions highlight the great divide that separates lay Bible readers from scholars, and the kinds of issues that motivate and excite each group.

This book attempts to bridge that divide by offering an informed, scholarly introduction to certain topics—from the location of the Garden of Eden to the identification of the Shroud of Turin—that seem to be of perpetual fascination to lay readers.

The aim is not to debunk or demystify: Indeed, one chapter recounts the rediscovery of one of the long-lost rivers of Eden; another identifies the Star of Bethlehem with a historical celestial event—a rare conjunction of Jupiter and Saturn in 7 B.C.—and explains why the magi, wise men from the East, would have interpreted this as the sign of a new, divinely appointed king.

The greatest challenge for anyone trying to "solve" a Biblical mystery is that the Bible interweaves the historical and the theological, the mystical and the verifiable—often in one sentence. A fabulous wooden boat, large enough to hold two of every species of animal on earth, lands atop a well-known mountain range in what is now eastern Turkey. Four rivers flow from Eden—the famed Tigris and Euphrates and the equally obscure Gihon and Pishon. Are the latter real bodies of water whose names have been lost to time? Did the Biblical writers deliberately obfuscate their identity so that no one could ever find Eden? Or are they all mythical rivers?

Another challenge is that Biblical mysteries often involve miracles, about which modern Bible readers have wide-ranging views. While many accept miracle stories at face value, some see them as allegories. Still others find assurance in coming up with naturalistic explanations—a tidal wave parted the Red Sea, or a comet hovered above Bethlehem when Jesus was born—for events that must have seemed miraculous to the Biblical authors.

The essays in this volume approach these issues in varying ways. Yet each must grapple with the question of what modern scholarship can and cannot tell us about the Biblical world, how the Bible can and cannot be read as a history book, which questions we can hope to answer—and which mysteries must remain mysteries.

Molly Dewsnap Meinhardt

About the Authors

Emmanuel Anati is founder and executive director of the Centro Camuno di Studi Preistorici in Capo di Ponte, Italy, and professor ordinarius (retired) of palaeo-ethnology at the University of Lecce in Italy. He has directed the archaeological survey of Har Karkom since 1980.

Israel Finkelstein is professor of archaeology at Tel Aviv University and the codirector of the Megiddo expedition. He co-wrote *The Bible Unearthed* (Free Press, 2001).

Rivka Gonen is an archaeologist and a former curator of Jewish ethnography at the Israel Museum.

Howard W. Goodkind formerly served as editor-in-chief at Prentice-Hall and chairman of the board of Encyclopedia Britannica.

Hillel Halkin, a writer based in Israel, has translated numerous works of Hebrew and Yiddish literature.

Ronald S. Hendel is professor of Hebrew Bible in the Department of Near Eastern Studies at the University of California, Berkeley. His book *Remembering Abraham: Culture, Memory, and History in the Hebrew Bible* is forthcoming from Oxford University Press.

Ephraim Isaac is director of the Institute of Semitic Studies at Princeton University. An expert in both Jewish and Ethiopian religious traditions, he held the first professorship in Harvard's Afro-American Studies program.

Allen Kerkeslager is assistant professor of New Testament at St. Joseph's University in Philadelphia. A specialist in the study of ancient Judaism and early Christianity, he focuses his writings mainly on Judaism in Greco-Roman Egypt, with a particular emphasis on first-century Alexandria.

Simo Parpola is professor of Assyriology at the University of Helsinki. He has translated and published the correspondence of Sargon II from the Babylonian state archives.

Bezalel Porten is a professor at the Institute of Jewish Studies at the Hebrew University. The leading expert on the Elephantine papyri, Porten is currently preparing a revised edition of his *Archives from Elephantine*, to be published by Brill.

James Sauer was a curator and research associate at Harvard's Semitic Museum. An expert in the archaeology of Jordan and Yemen, he died in 1999.

Hershel Shanks is the founder and editor of *Biblical Archaeology Review*, *Bible Review* and *Archaeology Odyssey*, and the author of several popular books on the Dead Sea Scrolls, Jerusalem and archaeology.

Suzanne F. Singer is former managing editor of *Biblical Archaeology Review*, *Bible Review* and *Moment*. She is now a contributing editor for the magazines and divides her time between Jerusalem and Washington, D.C.

William Stiebing is an archaeologist and history professor at the University of New Orleans. He recently published *Ancient Near Eastern History and Culture* (Longman, 2003).

Robert A. Wild, S.J., is president of Marquette University, where he formerly taught New Testament and theology.

Ben Witherington III is professor of New Testament at Asbury Theological Seminary in Lexington, Kentucky. He recently published *The Gospel Code: Novel Claims about Jesus, Mary Magdalene and Da Vinci* (Intervarsity, 2004).

"A river flows out of Eden to water the garden, and from there it divides and becomes four branches. The name of the first is Pishon; it is the one that flows around the whole land of Havilah, where there is gold; and the gold of that land is good; bdellium and onyx stone are there. The name of the second river is Gihon; it is the one that flows around the whole land of Cush. The name of the third river is Tigris, which flows east of Assyria. And the fourth river is the Euphrates."

(Genesis 2:10-14)

Part I

EDEN

The name Eden is believed to mean "well-watered place" or "delight," and the Book of Genesis paints a tantalizing picture of the four-branched river that flowed from the lush garden. The detailed description in Genesis 2 includes the names of each branch and lists the minerals abundant in the surrounding region. Based on this textual map, many have striven to locate the source of the river: the Garden itself. But it has proved challenging. While two of the rivers, the Tigris and Euphrates, are located in modern Iraq and go by the same names today, the identity of the Gihon and the Pishon remains uncertain. Because the Gihon is said to run "around the whole land of Cush" (modern Ethiopia), some modern scholars identify it with the Nile. Others have speculated that the Gihon should be associated instead with the Gihon Spring in Jerusalem, a relatively small but essential water source for the earliest residents of the city.

Havilah, the mineral-rich region through which the Pishon flows, is often identified with southern Arabia, where gold is abundant. But attempts to positively identify the Pishon with any one river in this area have failed. In the accompanying chapter, James Sauer offers an earthly reason for this failure: For thousands of years, the river has been hidden by the desert sands of Arabia; a poor understanding of how different the climate was in ancient times has discouraged anyone from looking for a river in this modern wasteland. Sauer finds that a better understanding of early climate changes not only helps locate the Pishon River but also provides a backdrop for the floods and famines of the Bible.

CHAPTER 1

A Lost River of Eden

Rediscovering the Pishon

James Sauer

Evidence of climatic change has the potential of changing Biblical history as we know it. It could help date the patriarchal age, the sojourn in Egypt (the Joseph story) and the origins of the Flood story. It may even enable us to locate at least one of the four rivers associated with the Garden of Eden.[1]

Until very recently, the prevailing assumption among scholars had been that the climate of the Near East changed little, if at all, after about 9000 B.C.E.,* or the end of the last glacial period. This concept of climate stability has been held by the vast majority of scholars working in the Near East, including such leading Israeli archaeologists as the late Yohanan Aharoni[2] and Amihai Mazar.[3] But in the last few years, this consensus has begun to shift, thanks to the work of such scholars as Aharon Horowitz,[4] Thomas Levy,[5] Paul Goldberg and Arlene M. Rosen.[6] My own work is simply an extension of theirs.

---

*B.C.E. (Before the Common Era) and C.E. (Common Era) are common academic designations for the eras more commonly known as B.C. (Before Christ) and A.D. (*Anno Domini*).

The evidence is unfortunately quite complex and technical, so here I will only summarize it, giving some examples.[7] The bottom line is that climatic changes have occurred in historic periods in the Near East; these climatic changes, which may explain widespread social changes, appear to have been a significant part of the Biblical memory.

Much of our evidence comes from soil samples taken by drilling deep holes, called boreholes, into the earth. Three boreholes, two from Israel's Hula Lake (drained at the turn of the century and now partially refilled) and the other from the Mediterranean coast of Israel, provide us with pollen samples from various periods.[8] This is important because a high percentage of arboreal (tree) pollen is evidence of a once-dense forest cover, which in turn indicates a period of heavy rainfall.

The three borehole samples from Israel indicate percentages of arboreal pollen were markedly higher (indicating a wetter

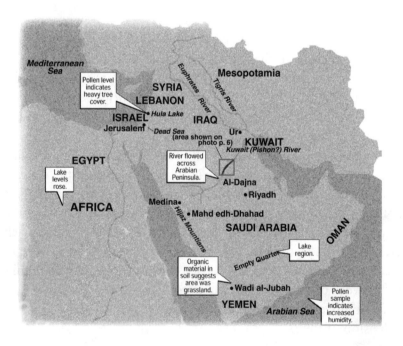

Evidence from throughout the Near East indicates that this region underwent a wet period from about 7500 to 3500 B.C.E.

phase) in the Chalcolithic period (c. 4500-3500 B.C.E.), which ended with a dry oscillation before a wetter Early Bronze Age I (c. 3500-2850 B.C.E.), a somewhat drier but still moist phase during Early Bronze II to III (c. 2850-2350 B.C.E.) and a more arid phase in at least part of the Early Bronze IV period (c. 2350-2000 B.C.E.; called by some Middle Bronze I). This aridity peaks in Early Bronze IV. Middle Bronze Age I-II (c. 2000-1550 B.C.E.) witnesses a return to much wetter conditions, tapering off gradually through the Late Bronze Age (c. 1550-1200 B.C.E.) and the Iron Age (1200-586 B.C.E.). A slight increase in moisture appears in the Byzantine period (324-638 C.E.) and Islamic period (beginning in 638 C.E.), continuing until about 1400 C.E., and then declining until modern times.[9]

A wetter Chalcolithic period than we had previously supposed correlates beautifully with other evidence from Chalcolithic sites in Jordan and southern Israel. Teleilat el-Ghassul in the southeastern Jordan Valley and sites like Beersheba and Shiqmim in southern Israel are located in topographically low areas with little rainfall in modern times (generally between 0 and 200 millimeters annually). These sites (located in what is known as steppe-desert) must have had more rainfall when they were occupied. Toward the end of the Chalcolithic period, however, there was a marked drop in arboreal pollens resulting from a decline in wooded vegetation, which indicates a decrease in rainfall.

My own studies in Yemen buttress this evidence.[10] In Wadi al-Jubah, we found dark paleosol (ancient soil), in places nearly 10 feet thick. This contrasts to the light, dry soil associated with arid climates. Studies of this dark soil revealed that it was full of decayed organic matter such as roots—a product of wetter conditions. We were able to date the layer of paleosol by carbon-14 tests. The test results show that the wetter period extended to the end of the Chalcolithic period, about 3500 B.C.E. After that, a drier period (but one still wetter than today) probably followed.

Similarly, in southern Saudi Arabia ancient lakes existed in the Empty Quarter until about 3500 B.C.E. Today, the Empty Quarter is the largest sand desert in the world.

A core sample from the Arabian Sea not far from Yemen gave clear evidence of a wetter environment from about 7000 to

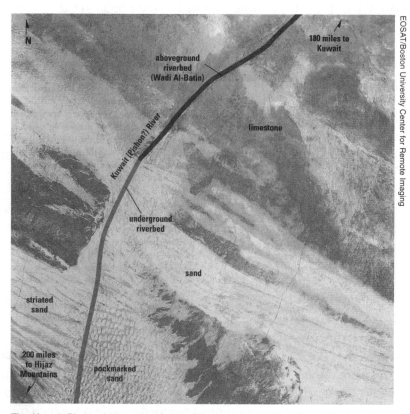

The Kuwait River, which author James Sauer cautiously identifies as the long-lost Pishon, once cut across the entire Arabian peninsula. Although much of the riverbed lies under desert sand today, its course can be traced on this satellite photo.

The region shown in the photo is marked with a square on the map on page 4. Dark areas in the photo indicate limestone; lighter areas denote desert sand. It is easy to detect the dry riverbed (today called Wadi Al-Batin) cutting through the limestone at top center. The riverbed appears to peter out as it reaches the sand (at center).

Note, however, that when the line of the river is extended across the sand dunes, as shown in the drawing, the desert sand dunes to the right (southeast) appear pockmarked; those to the left (northeast) are striated. Sand patterns like these are created by the circulation of the air in the desert, which in turn is influenced by the topography. That is, something beneath the sand is creating the variations in the sand. Boston University geologist Farouk El-Baz determined that that something was a major underground river that ran along a fault line.

El-Baz had been studying satellite photos of the Arabian peninsula to determine how great quantities of basalt and granite pebbles, stones indigenous to western Arabia, had ended up in Kuwait. He determined that the long-lost river—now half covered by sand—had dragged the stones down from the Hijaz mountains and dumped them in the form of pebbles along a fan-shaped delta, which covered about two-thirds of modern Kuwait.

5000 B.C.E., followed by what appears to have been a drier climate after about 3000 B.C.E.[11] Other consistent evidence comes from African lakes.[12]

Some especially striking but very different kind of evidence comes from the Arabian Peninsula. With the use of remote sensing technology, Boston University geologist Farouk El-Baz has traced a major, partially underground, sand river channel from the mountains of Hijaz to Kuwait, which he has named the Kuwait River. Dated by associated geology, the dry river channel is clearly a relic of a wetter phase in Arabia during this period. It gradually dried up sometime after 3500 B.C.E.[13]

All this evidence (and much more that I have not cited here) supports the view that a global wet phase began around 7500 B.C.E. This phase, though probably interrupted by some drier periods, was predominantly wet until at least 3500 B.C.E., around the end of the Chalcolithic period. Water filled major lakes, at least one river flowed in Arabia and part of Arabia was grassland.

The wet phase in Mesopotamia in the mid-fourth millennium B.C.E. is probably associated with Biblical and other ancient Near Eastern traditions of floods. We have no evidence of a global, catastrophic flood, however, but of several localized floods. In the early 20th century, British archaeologist Leonard Woolley discovered at Ur an 8-foot-thick sterile layer that he originally considered evidence of the Flood, though he eventually abandoned that viewpoint because the level in question dated too early. Later flood deposits were subsequently found at higher levels at several sites.[14]

The Kuwait River probably has a more direct Biblical connection. It may well be the Pishon River, one of the four rivers, according to the Bible, associated with Eden:

> The name of the first is Pishon; it is the one that flows around the whole land of Havilah, where there is gold; and the gold of that land is good; bdellium and onyx stone are there.

Genesis 2:11-12

Although the meaning of some of the details in this passage is uncertain, it does seem to describe a river flowing into the head of the Persian Gulf from the low mountains of western Arabia, the path followed by the recently discovered Kuwait River. An important key is the Biblical phrase "the gold of that land is good." Only one place in Arabia has such a deposit—the famous site of Mahd edh-Dhahab, the "Cradle of Gold."[15] This ancient and modern gold mining site is located about 125 miles south of Medina, near the headwaters of the Kuwait River.

"Well, of course, it's the Flood," Lady Woolley casually remarked when her husband's excavation team uncovered an 8-foot-thick layer of soil at Ur that contained no evidence of human activity, sandwiched between two layers of pottery. In the photo above, two Arab workmen stand beside part of what came to be known as "the Flood deposit."

Woolley later retracted his identification of the Flood stratum, arguing that the deposit, which he dated to the mid-fourth millennium B.C.E., was too old to have resulted from the Biblical Deluge. Nevertheless, it offers strong evidence of flooding during the regional wet period that may have inspired the Genesis Flood story.

The Biblical text also mentions bdellium and onyx. Aromatic resins such as bdellium are known in Yemen to the southwest, and, although they are not thought to have been produced in the vicinity of Medina, they could easily have been brought there. Semiprecious stones such as alabaster also come from these areas, but it is uncertain whether other precious stones, such as onyx, do.

In any event, no other river would seem to fit the Biblical description. I am therefore inclined to think that the Kuwait River could well be the Pishon of the Bible. If so, it implies extraordinary memory on the part of the Biblical authors, since the river dried up sometime between about 3500 and 2000 B.C.E.

Our knowledge of climatic change can also help explain dramatic social change. For example, at the end of the third millennium B.C.E., say around 2000 B.C.E., most major urban sites in Israel and Jordan were abandoned for about 300 years. As Arlene Rosen has persuasively argued, a period of great aridity occurred at the end of the third millennium B.C.E.[16] Harvey Weiss has similarly demonstrated that, in northern Syria, the climate was drier from about 2200 to 1900 B.C.E., suggesting that the cultural collapse at the beginning of that period may have been caused primarily by prolonged drought.

In Egypt, historical records attest to serious famines in this same period.

The aridity of this period may also explain some of the shifts in settlement in Israel and Jordan as well as in Syria, Mesopotamia and Egypt.

In my opinion, the descriptions of the severe famines at the time of Joseph (Genesis 41-47) reflect this period of aridity. The famine reported at the time of Joseph is probably another accurate fragment of climatic memory reflected in the early Biblical traditions.

If this is correct, we may place the patriarchal age sometime in the third millennium B.C.E. Proceeding from these considerations is the likely conclusion that the Early Bronze Age sites of Bab edh-Dhra, Numeira and other places adjacent to the Dead Sea in Jordan were indeed some of the Biblical Cities of the Plain (Genesis 14). This argument was made early on by the excavators but has since been disregarded.[17]

I do not mean to imply that the early Biblical stories are literally true. Clearly, the Biblical traditions are very much cast in the worldview of the Iron Age. But that has led too many scholars to ignore the possibility that the Biblical texts preserve many older traditions. Since the memories of climatic change and of early geography seem so accurate, some of these traditions might have been written down for the first time, not in the tenth century B.C.E. (the earliest date given by most scholars), but very much earlier.

These conclusions not only agree with the views of the great Biblical archaeologist William F. Albright, but they also push back even further his dates for the historical backgrounds of the Biblical traditions. He and his students opted for a Patriarchal Age in the Middle Bronze period, shortly after 2000 B.C.E. The evidence I have just presented would place it in the Early Bronze period. Bible scholar David Noel Freedman was right, but for the wrong reasons, when he proposed a third-millennium B.C.E. date for the patriarchs.

I thus disagree with archaeologists like William Dever in their treatment of the Bronze Age and the preceding Chalcolithic period. I think we can expect more archaeological, climatic, geographical, literary and artistic evidence from these periods that will buttress my position. "Biblical archaeology" can and should be extended back to these periods and to regions as far afield as Mesopotamia and Egypt, as Albright originally maintained.

1. I thank Dr. Lawrence E. Stager for my research associate position at the Harvard Semitic Museum. The funding to support this research came from Richard J. Scheuer, Eugene M. Grant, Leon Levy, Shelby White and P.E. MacAlister. Thanks to Dr. Lawrence T. Geraty, the president of La Sierra University in Riverside, California, this university has provided the institutional base for these donations.

2. Yohanan Aharoni, *The Archaeology of the Land of Israel* (Philadelphia: Westminster, 1982).

3. Amihai Mazar, *Archaeology of the Land of the Bible, 10,000-586 B.C.E.* (New York: Doubleday, 1990).

4. Aharon Horowitz, "Climatic and Vegetational Developments in Northeastern Israel During Upper Pleistocene-Holocene Times," in *Pollen et Spores* 13 (1971), pp. 255-278; "Preliminary Palynological Indications as to the Climate of Israel During the Last 6,000 Years," in *Paleorient 2* (1974), pp. 407-414; "Human Settlement Patterns in Israel," in *Expedition* 20:4 (1978), pp. 55-58; and *The Quaternary of Israel* (New York: Academic Press, 1979).

5. Thomas E. Levy, "The Chalcolithic Period," in *Biblical Archaeologist* 49 (1986), pp. 82-108.

6. Paul Goldberg and Arlene M. Rosen, "Early Holocene Palaeoenvironments of Israel," in *Shiqmim 1: Studies Concerning Chalcolithic Societies in the Northern Negev Desert, Israel* (1982-1984), British Archaeological Reports International Series 356:i-ii (1987), ed. Thomas E. Levy, pp. 23-33.

7. For details, see James A. Sauer, "A New Climatic and Archaeological View of the Early Biblical Traditions," in *Scripture and Other Artifacts*, eds. Michael D. Coogan et al. (Louisville, KY: Westminster/John Knox, 1994).

8. See Horowitz, "Human Settlement Patterns," figure 1.

9. Interestingly, the decline after 1400 C.E. has sometimes been attributed to Ottoman tax policies or unregulated wood cutting, but in fact the process began even earlier, with a period of greater aridity in Late Mamluk times.

10. See Sauer and J.A. Blakely, "Archaeology Along the Spice Route of Yemen," in *Araby the Blest*, ed. Daniel T. Potts (Copenhagen: Carsten Niebuhr Institute, 1988), pp. 90-115.

11. F. Sirocko, M. Sarnthein, H. Erlenkeuser, H. Lange, M. Arnold and J.C. Duplessy, "Century-Scale Events in Monsoonal Climate over the Past 24,000 Years," in *Nature* 364 (1993), pp. 322-364.

12. Karl W. Butzer, Glynn L. Isaac, Jonathan L. Richardson and Celia Washbourn-Kamau, "Radiocarbon Dating of East African Lake Levels," in *Science* 175 (1972), pp. 1069-1076.

13. See Farouk El-Baz, "Boston University Scientist Discovers Ancient River System in Saudi Arabia," in *Boston University News*, March 25, 1993, pp. 1-2; and "Gulf War Disruption of the Desert Surface in Kuwait," in *Gulf War and the Environment* (New York: Gordon and Breach, 1994).

14. See Max E.L. Mallowan, "Noah's Flood Reconsidered," in *Iraq* 26 (1964), plate 20, pp. 62-82.

15. See Lois Berkowitz, "Has the U.S. Geological Service Found King Solomon's Mines?" *Biblical Archaeology Review (BAR)* 3:3 (September 1977).

16. Arlene M. Rosen, "Environmental Change at the End of the Early Bronze Age," in *L'urbanisation de la Palestine à l'age du Bronze ancien*, British Archaeological Reports International Series 527 (1989), ed. Pierre de Miroschedji, pp. 247-256.

17. See "Have Sodom and Gomorrah Been Found?" *BAR* 6:5 (September/October 1985); also see Walter E. Rast and Richard T. Schaub, "Survey of the Southeastern Plain of the Dead Sea 1973," in *Annual of the Department of Antiquities of Jordan* 19 (1974), pp. 5-53; "The Southeastern Dead Sea Plain Expedition: An Interim Report of the 1977 Season," in *Annual of the American Schools of Oriental Research* 46 (1981); "Preliminary Report of the 1981 Expedition to the Dead Sea Plain, Jordan," in *Bulletin of the American Schools of Oriental Research* 254 (1984), pp. 35-60; and "Reports of the Expedition to the Dead Sea Plain, Jordan 1, " in *Bab edh-Dhra: Excavations in the Cemetery Directed by Paul W. Lapp* (1965-1967) (Winona Lake, IN: Eisenbrauns, 1989); see also Michael D. Coogan, "Numeira 1981," in the *Bulletin of the American Schools of Oriental Research* 255 (1984), pp. 75-81.

"But God remembered Noah and all the wild animals and all the domestic animals that were with him in the Ark. And God made a wind blow over the earth, and the waters subsided; the fountains of the deep and the windows of the heavens were closed, the rain from the heavens was restrained, and the waters gradually receded from the earth. At the end of one hundred fifty days, the waters had abated; and in the seventh month, on the seventeenth day of the month, the Ark came to rest on the mountains of Ararat."

(Genesis 8:1-4)

Part II

Noah's Ark

The apparent precision of the Biblical account in naming the mountain on which the Ark came to rest has inspired seekers to search for the remains of Noah's Ark on Mt. Ararat in eastern Turkey. In truth, the Biblical account does not mention just one peak but a range of mountains—the Ararats, we might call them. But Biblical geography is the least of the problems facing the modern quester, who must first explain the relationship of the Biblical account to remarkably similar but much older Mesopotamian accounts of an Ark and a Deluge.

Chapter 2

A Futile Quest
The Search for Noah's Ark

William H. Stiebing, Jr.

———•◦•———

Throughout history, numerous searchers have sought the remains of Noah's Ark on the rocky peaks of Mt. Ararat, in eastern Turkey, but, as we shall see, no conclusive evidence of the Ark has been found. In modern times, these efforts have been restricted because of internal problems in Turkey, the Greco-Turkish conflict in Cyprus and Turkish sensitivity to foreign expeditions on Mt. Ararat, which overlooks both the Iranian and the former Soviet borders (see map, p. 22). Nevertheless, many people remain confident that the Ark is still on the slopes of Ararat, waiting to be found.

The story of Noah and the Great Flood is one of the best known tales from the Bible, and has long been a source of contention. Ever since the 17th century and the beginnings of modern geology, prehistoric archaeology and evolutionary theory, some scholars have challenged the scientific and historical validity of the early chapters of Genesis—especially the accounts of the Creation and the Flood. Others, convinced that the Bible is the literal Word of God, verbally inspired and inerrant, have sought to prove that the Genesis version of man's early history is correct.

Archaeology has played a somewhat ambivalent role in this debate. In Europe during the 18th and 19th centuries, human artifacts and skeletal remains were found associated with the fossils of extinct animals in a number of places. These finds led antiquarians and geologists to abandon the widely accepted chronology that the 17th-century archbishop James Ussher of Armagh, Ireland, had worked out based on the Biblical accounts. According to Ussher's calculations, the Creation of the world had taken place in 4004 B.C. and the Great Flood had occurred in 2348 B.C. These dates were printed in the margins of some editions of the Bible, and in the minds of many they had assumed an authority and sanctity virtually as great as that of the Biblical text itself. But evidence of the extreme antiquity of man could not be easily reconciled with the very short chronology suggested by the Scriptures. Thus, discoveries in European prehistory contributed to skeptical and scientific attacks on the validity of Genesis.

Turkish Culture and Tourism Office, Washington, D.C.

The 17,000-foot peak of Mt. Ararat (Turkish, Büyük Agri Dagi) dominates the mountainous region of eastern Turkey.

On the other hand, a number of early archaeological discoveries in the Near East tended to confirm the accuracy of Biblical accounts. Since many assumed the unity of Biblical teaching—either it was all true or it was all false—finds verifying accounts in the Book of Kings were often cited as proof of the historicity of the Bible as a whole. Much of the public interest in and financial support for 19th- and early-20th-century Near Eastern excavations came from individuals and groups intent on verifying Biblical history.

In 1872, George Smith, an assistant in the Assyrian section of the British Museum, made a discovery that raised the debate to a new level. He had been sorting and classifying cuneiform tablets found at Kuyunjik (ancient Nineveh) (see map, p. 22) by earlier British excavators when suddenly his attention was seized by a line in a broken text that seemed to be part of a myth or legend. The sentence read, "On Mount Nisir the ship landed; Mount Nisir held the ship fast, allowing no motion." Hurriedly Smith glanced down the rest of the column and read:

When the seventh day arrived,
I sent forth a dove—I released it.
The dove went away, but came back;
Since no resting-place appeared, she returned.
Then I sent forth a swallow—I released it.
The swallow went away, but came back;
Since no resting-place appeared, she returned.
Then I sent forth a raven—I released it.
The raven went away, and seeing that the waters had diminished,
She ate, circled, cawed and did not return.

Smith knew at once that he had found a Mesopotamian version of the Biblical story of the Deluge.

There was a gap in the text that could not be filled by any of the tablets in the museum. But when Smith reported his discovery in a paper read before the Society of Biblical Archaeology, so great was the public interest that the London *Daily Telegraph* offered to equip an expedition to Nineveh to search for the missing tablets. In May 1873 Smith arrived at Kuyunjik and began sifting through the debris piled up by previous British expeditions. He found over 300 fragments of tablets that had been unnoticed and discarded by earlier excavators—a sad commentary on the archaeological methodology of the time. Among the texts he recovered was a tablet containing the missing portion of the Mesopotamian flood story.

The flood account found by Smith proved to be part of a seventh-century B.C. Assyrian copy of the *Epic of Gilgamesh*.[1] But fragmentary copies of the same work dating from the middle of the second millennium B.C. have since been found in the ruins of the Hittite capital at Boghazkoy. Portions of an Old

Babylonian version of this epic (c. 1900-1600 B.C.) have also been discovered. However, even without the early fragments of the *Epic of Gilgamesh*, Assyriologists knew from the language of Smith's tablets that the story belonged to an era long before the seventh century B.C. Internal linguistic evidence indicates that the *Epic of Gilgamesh* and the flood story it contains must have been composed near the beginning of the Old Babylonian Period, c. 1900-1800 B.C.—more than 500 years before the Hebrew Exodus from Egypt.

The Babylonian-Assyrian flood story in the Gilgamesh Epic is so similar to the Hebrew account in Genesis that it was clear that the two must be related in some way. A number of scholars argued that the Biblical narrative must have been derived from the earlier Mesopotamian legend. This view became even more persuasive in 1914 when Arno Poebel published a very fragmentary Sumerian account of the Flood. The tablet containing this account had been unearthed in the University of Pennsylvania's excavations at Nippur between 1889 and 1900. The text was so badly damaged that only limited portions of the story survived: the gods' decision to send the Flood, the warning to Ziusudra (the Sumerian Noah) to build a large boat, the coming of the Flood, Ziusudra's sacrifice of thanksgiving after the Flood, and the deification of Ziusudra. Enough remained, however, to indicate that the Sumerian flood story originally contained most elements of the Old Babylonian version found in the *Epic of Gilgamesh*.[2]

The Sumerians were non-Semitic inhabitants of southern Mesopotamia who first invented the cuneiform script, used widely in the ancient Near East, and who created the earliest civilization known at present. Their culture was dominant in Mesopotamia from about 3500 to 2400 B.C. Though conquered by the Semitic ruler Sargon of Akkad (c. 2371-2316 B.C.), they continued to play an important role in Mesopotamian affairs until the end of the 18th century B.C. Most of the Sumerian literary texts from Nippur, including the flood tablet, were found in the archaeological layer belonging to the time of the Third Dynasty of Ur and the Isin-Larsa Period (c. 2113-1800 B.C.), but the myths the tablets record are almost certainly much older. They reflect social and governmental institutions which had disappeared among the Sumerians long before the beginning of the second millennium B.C. Thus, it is thought that an original Sumerian flood story provided the inspiration for the various Old Babylonian accounts (which in turn served as the models for the Assyrian versions).

The discovery of this Sumerian flood narrative confirmed the great antiquity of the flood tradition in Mesopotamia, and convinced most scholars that the Biblical story of Noah must have had a Mesopotamian origin. But others claimed that the Mesopotamian flood stories proved the historicity of the Biblical Deluge. Supporters of this view argued that the similarities between the Biblical narrative and the account of the *Epic of Gilgamesh* were not evidence of literary or intellectual dependence, but rather indicated that the two traditions were independent accounts of the same historical event—a great worldwide Flood from which only one human family had been saved. The Genesis account was taken to be an accurate record of what had occurred, while the various Mesopotamian stories were thought to be derived from a tradition which, though originally accurate, had gradually become debased by polytheism and riddled with factual errors.

Then in 1929 more fuel was added to the controversy by Leonard Woolley's discoveries at Ur in southern Mesopotamia. Workmen digging a pit through the prehistoric Ubaid strata reached what they thought to be virgin soil. But since the level of the "virgin soil" was not as deep as Woolley had expected it to be, he ordered the workmen to continue the excavation. After digging through 8 feet of clean, water-laid mud containing no artifacts, the men suddenly encountered Ubaid painted pottery and flint implements once more. Woolley called over two members of his staff and asked for their explanation of the deposits. He recounts that "they did not know what to say. My wife came along and looked and was asked the same question, and she turned away remarking casually, 'Well, of course, it's the Flood.' That was the right answer."[3]

Woolley thought he had found evidence of the Great Flood that lay behind the Mesopotamian traditions. This flood had not been a universal Deluge, he argued, but it had covered most of Mesopotamia—the "whole world" to the prehistoric people who had lived there. In his opinion, the Biblical story of Noah had been derived from the Mesopotamian flood accounts. Many people cited Woolley's finds as proof that a worldwide flood had occurred, just as Genesis said. Their conviction was strengthened when over the next few years flood layers were reported from Kish, Fara and Nineveh, three other sites in Mesopotamia.

This archaeological "evidence" of the Flood was widely publicized and found its way into many popular works on Biblical archaeology. However, as Professor John Bright demonstrated in a 1942 article,[4] the archaeological discoveries in the Near East do not support Woolley's interpretation, much less that of some of his popularizers. Mounds in Syria and Palestine (such as Jericho) which exhibit fairly continuous occupation since at least 5000 or 4500 B.C. show no signs of destruction by a Great Flood. Even in Mesopotamia, most sites (including al-'Ubaid near Ur) have produced no evidence of "the Flood." At those sites where flood deposits have been found, the date of the flood varies widely. The Ur flood layer was in the middle of Ubaid remains (in southern Mesopotamia the Ubaid Period dates from c. 4500 to 3500 B.C.); at Kish, the flood occurred in the Early Dynastic Period (c. 2900-2400 B.C.); at Fara, the alluvial deposit was between the Jemdet Nasr (or Protoliterate C-D, c. 3100-2900 B.C.) and Early Dynastic layers; and the flood layer at Nineveh separates remains of the Halaf Period (c. 5000-4300 B.C.) from those of the Ubaid (c. 4300-3500 B.C. in northern Mesopotamia). Thus, the flood layers at various Mesopotamian sites are the results of different local floods which were no doubt quite common in that area. They cannot be used as evidence of The Flood of Mesopotamian tradition or of Genesis. Even at Woolley's Ur, the flood evidence he found did not cover the entire site!

Since World War II many believers in the historicity of the Genesis Flood have centered their hopes on expeditions to Mt. Ararat, located in extreme eastern Turkey (see map, p. 22). Actually, the Bible does not name this mountain as the one on which Noah landed. Genesis 8:4 merely specifies the region where the Ark came to rest—"the mountains of Ararat," or, as the New English Bible translates it, "a mountain in Ararat." Ararat is the Biblical name for Urartu as this area was known to the Assyrians. This mountainous region, centered around Lake Van, was later called Armenia, but now it is divided between Turkey, Armenia,

Iran and Iraq. Armenian tradition, however, has long identified
Mt. Ararat as the peak on which the Ark landed.

Mt. Ararat stands in almost solitary splendor, rising to a
height of over 16,900 feet above sea level and providing a relief of
almost 14,000 feet between its summit and the plains at its base.
Since Mt. Ararat is much higher than other mountains in the
area, its peak would be the first to emerge above receding waters
if the whole region were submerged by a vast Flood. This fact
probably explains its traditional designation as the landing place
of the Ark—although the Biblical account does not suggest that
the Ark came to rest on the highest mountain of the region.

"Arkeologists" (as the searchers for the Ark have come to be
called, by themselves as well as by others) provide a number of
pieces of "evidence" to support their conviction that Noah's Ark
has survived the centuries atop Mt. Ararat:[5]

- Ancient historians such as Berossus (a Babylonian priest of
  the third century B.C. whose account of Mesopotamian
  history in Greek has survived only in fragmentary quotations by other ancient writers) and Josephus (a Jewish historian of the first century A.D.) mention reports that the
  Ark still existed in their respective eras. Also, medieval
  travelers such as Marco Polo testify that Armenians of that
  day claimed that the Ark was still on Mt. Ararat.

- Shortly before his death in 1920, an Armenian-born
  American is supposed to have told friends that in 1856
  three atheistic British scientists hired him and his father
  to guide them up Mt. Ararat to prove that the Ark was
  not there. When the boy and his father led the scientists
  directly to the Ark, the scientists threatened them with
  death if they ever reported the incident. Soon after
  World War I a British scientist is supposed to have
  admitted in a deathbed confession that he was one of the
  three atheists who by death threats had suppressed their
  guides from divulging the fact of the Ark's existence on
  Mt. Ararat. This deathbed confession is supposed to have
  been widely reported in many newspapers of the time.
  However, no one has ever been able to find copies of
  these articles or to identify the individuals involved.

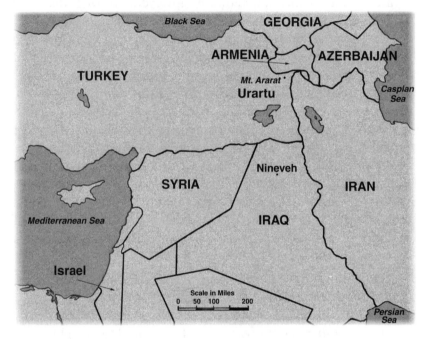

- In 1876 Sir James Bryce, a British explorer, found a large piece of hand-tooled wood at the 13,000-foot level of Mt. Ararat.

- In 1883 a group of Turkish commissioners, checking avalanche conditions on the mountain, are said to have found the Ark and entered it. But no one believed them.

- A Russian aviator supposedly spotted the Ark from the air in 1915 and an expedition was sent to investigate. The Russian soldiers located and explored the ship, but before they could return to St. Petersburg, the Russian Revolution of 1917 occurred. The records of the expedition were lost and the members scattered, but some relatives and friends later reported having heard their story.

- About 1937 a New Zealand archaeologist named Hardwicke Knight was making his way around the mountain near the snow line when he saw what appeared to be heavy timbers projecting from the ice field. Only later did he realize that these may have been part of the Ark.

- During World War II both American and Russian aviators are supposed to have seen the Ark from the air. The Russians even took photographs that are reputed to have appeared in various U.S. papers. The story of one of the American sightings was supposedly reported in a 1943 Tunisian theatre edition of the Army paper *Stars and Stripes*. However, the articles and photographs cannot now be located.

- In 1953 George Greene, a geologist, took six aerial photographs of an object he believed to be the Ark. He died in 1962 and no trace of his unpublished photographs has been found, though several witnesses claim to have seen them.

- A large piece of hand-worked timber was pulled from a water-filled pocket deep in a crevasse on Ararat by Fernand Navarra in 1955. The partly fossilized wood was dated to about 3000 B.C. by a Spanish laboratory (primarily on the basis of its color and the extent of fossilization), but two independent carbon-14 tests by British and American laboratories have indicated a date around 450-750 A.D.[6]

- An orbiting U.S. Earth Resources Technology Satellite has taken photographs of Mt. Ararat which show a number of dark spots in the ice fields. One of these anomalies may represent the remains of Noah's Ark.

Even noncritical readers will note that most of the above "evidence" rests on hearsay that cannot be verified by objective means. Some of it is also inherently improbable. If the exact site of the Ark had been known from antiquity down through the Middle Ages, as Berossus, Josephus and Marco Polo state, is it likely that such a revered relic would have been subsequently lost and its precise location forgotten? (It should be noted that despite all the invasions, wars, and social turmoil in Palestine through the ages, the traditional locations of sacred places, once established, have been remembered and revered.) Is it believable that a threat by a pair of foreigners who lived thousands of miles away could have kept a believer silent about his discovery of Noah's Ark until he was near death more than 60 years later? And why is it that no one can now find copies of the articles and photographs that supposedly documented various modern discoveries of the Ark?

Only the wood found by Navarra and the anomalies on the satellite photographs are objective evidence, and they prove nothing. Man has lived around Mt. Ararat for many thousands of years, and for at least the last 17 centuries the natives of the area have regarded the mountain as the site where Noah's Ark landed. It would be very unusual if through the ages no buildings, monuments or other structures using wooden beams had ever been erected on the mountain near the edge of the snow field. Is the beam found by Navarra from the Ark or from some other manmade structure? If the carbon-14 dates are approximately correct, the wood is far too recent to come from the Ark. As for the anomalies in the satellite photographs, there are too many of them, and most represent areas too large for the Ark. It is much more likely that they represent natural features such as rock outcrops or small glacial lakes than manmade objects such as the Ark. In short, the so-called "evidence" for the existence of Noah's Ark on Mt. Ararat will convince only those who already believe and do not need to be convinced.

But granted that the evidence for the Ark's preservation is not very strong, why are most archaeologists so firmly convinced that the search for its remains is a waste of time and money? What makes them so sure that the Ark isn't somewhere on the slopes of Mt. Ararat?

First, of course, there are the logical and scientific objections to the Biblical story of the Flood. How could a vessel approximately 450 feet long, 75 feet wide and 45 feet high (Genesis 6:15; the Biblical cubit is about 18 inches long) hold two of every species of animal and bird (and seven pairs of each of the clean species) as well as provisions for a year? Some supporters of the story speculate that there may not have been as many species of animals in Noah's day as there are today and that the animals may have hibernated, eliminating their need for food.[7] However, Genesis 6:21 implies that the animals were to be fed normally during the time they were on the Ark, and, of course, not all species hibernate. Did God miraculously place all of the animals in a state of suspended animation? Those who accept the story as history see no reason why such miraculous intervention should be rejected, for the Flood itself, after all, is not a natural occurrence—it is a mighty act of God breaking into the course of human history. But the fact remains that the Bible does not mention (or even imply) any miracles in connection with the animals on the Ark.

Supporters of the Flood story claim that many geological features of the earth which would normally be explained as the work of millions of years (and thus contradict the relatively recent chronology of Genesis) were actually produced by the turbulent waters of the Flood. According to this theory, the earth's geography was quite different before the Flood, although it has not changed very much in the ages since. This theory presents its own problems: How did animals from the Ark get to Australia or the Americas after the Ark grounded on Ararat? More miracles not mentioned in the text must be posited.

To accept the Flood account as history one must not only forsake a logical (and even literal) interpretation of the text of Genesis, one must also abandon the principles and results of modern geology and prehistoric archaeology, both of which deny the existence of a universal Deluge during the span of man's history on earth.

A second major reason why archaeologists and Biblical scholars reject the quest for Noah's Ark lies in the Biblical text itself. Careful analysis of Genesis has shown that there is not one Biblical Flood story, but two. These two different accounts have been skillfully woven together to produce the composite story of the present text of Genesis, but stylistic differences as well as duplications and contradictions in the text have enabled scholars to identify the original versions. The earliest of these two accounts is that of the Yahwist (J), an unknown author who probably wrote during the tenth century B.C. This so-called J source includes Genesis 6:5-8, 7:1-5, 7-10, 12, 16b, 17b, 22-23 (though part of 7:9 is a gloss by the editor who wove the sources together), 8:2b, 3a, 6-12, 13b, 20-22. The second account is the product of the Exilic or early post-Exilic Priestly writer, known to scholars as P. This account consists of Genesis 6:9-22, 7:6, 11, 13-16a, 17a, 18-21, 24, 8:1-2a, 3b-5,13a, 14-19, and 9:1-17.[8]

The fact that these two Biblical accounts have so many elements in common that are not found in the Mesopotamian stories (such as Noah as the name of the hero, the two prologues stating that man's sin was the reason for the Flood, and the absence in both of any attempt to save craftsmen or the elements of man's civilization) points to their common origin in a tradition which we might call "proto-Israelite." But despite their common background, there are some significant differences between the accounts of J and P. In J, Noah saves seven pairs of every clean animal and one pair each of the unclean animals (7:2-3), while in P there is no distinction between clean and unclean creatures—one pair of each kind is taken aboard the Ark (6:19-20). J states that the Flood was caused by rainfall (7:4) and that it lasted 40 days (7:4, 12, 17; 8:6). However, P credits the Deluge to rainfall and a bursting forth of "the fountains of *tehom*" (the fountains or waters of the great abyss under the earth; Genesis 7:11, 8:2), and states that the Flood lasted for an entire year (7:24, 8:1,2a,3b-5,13a).

It is sometimes assumed that because P was written down much later than J, it must to some extent be dependent on J. However, this assumption is quite probably incorrect. The author of P seems to have been the recipient of a body of traditions that were preserved separately from those of J and that, though written down later, were often as ancient in origin. The differences between the Flood stories of J and P were probably the result of a common "proto-Israelite" Flood tradition being passed down in oral form among two different segments of the population or in two different areas of Palestine.

The similarities between the Biblical Flood stories and the Mesopotamian accounts (particularly the one in the *Epic of Gilgamesh*) are far greater than those between flood stories found in other parts of the world. Not only do both traditions refer to a universal Deluge of which one man is warned, escaping with his family and representatives of each animal species, but also both contain a divine command to make an Ark and to caulk it with bitumen, an account of the landing of the Ark on a mountain while the waters recede, the incident of the sending of the birds (a very close parallel), the building of an altar, and the offering of a sacrifice by the hero upon descent from the Ark. When all of these similarities are added to the fact that the phrase about the gods or God smelling the sweet savor of the sacrifice is virtually the same in each version, and that both stories come from the ancient Near East where widespread interrelations of peoples and cultures is demonstrable, the probability of these similarities being due to chance becomes almost zero.

Thus, it can be safely assumed that the Biblical Flood stories and the Mesopotamian traditions are related to one another, but it is impossible at present to reconstruct the exact relationship. How many (if any) intermediate versions stood between the "proto-Israelite" tradition and those of southern Mesopotamia we don't know. It is clear, though, that the Mesopotamian traditions have temporal priority and that they were the ultimate source of the Biblical versions.

The Genesis Flood stories, then, are legends, not history, and attempts to locate the remains of the Ark can result only in a waste of time and money. But the importance of the Biblical Flood narratives goes beyond the question of their historicity, for they testify to the convictions of the people who wrote them. Along with other material of mythical or legendary origin (Genesis 1-11, much of it also from Mesopotamia), the traditions about the Flood were used by the Biblical authors to form a prologue for the history of God's dealings with the people Israel. Although both J and P used material that was ultimately Mesopotamian in origin, the perspective from which they viewed their narratives was quite different from that of Mesopotamia. Historical experience had led the ancient Israelites to believe in an active, covenanting God who seeks to bind his people to Him. This belief was so strong that it not only colored the Israelite view of history, but it also transformed ancient myths and legends and made them an integral part of Israel's "salvation history."

According to the Biblical authors, the Flood was sent as a last resort when man had become so sinful that God could do nothing else. It was punishment for moral offenses, and it was deserved. But God, although just, is also a God of mercy, and upon seeing Noah's offering, he promised never to destroy mankind again (no matter how much man deserved it). Thus, the Flood story is used to add another part of the general backdrop against which Israel's "salvation history" would play out. When even the descendants of the faithful Noah go wrong, God calls a special family (which becomes a people) to serve him and become his instruments. The rest of the Old Testament describes Israel's struggle with that call.

Thus, looking at the perspective from which the Biblical writers viewed their Flood stories, and examining the context into which they placed those stories, one cannot help but feel that the Flood tradition has undergone a qualitative change since being removed from Mesopotamia. That the Old Testament contains mythological elements and that it preserved some legendary stories which originated in Mesopotamia or in other cultures of the ancient Near East is to be expected. What is surprising is the degree to which these myths and legends have been transformed by the ancient Israelite conviction that again and again throughout their history a voice has called to them saying:

> You are my witnesses...and my servant whom I have chosen,
> that you may know and believe me and understand that I am He.
> Before me no god was formed, nor shall there be any after me.
> I, I am Yahweh, and besides me there is no savior.
>
> Isaiah 43:10-11

1. See E.A. Speiser's translation of the epic in James B. Pritchard, ed., *Ancient Near Eastern Texts,* 2nd ed. (Princeton, NJ: Princeton Univ. Press, 1955), pp. 72-99, esp. pp. 93-95. See also pp. 104-106 for the fragments of the *Atrahasis Epic,* another Old Babylonian composition containing a flood account.

2. See Samuel Noah Kramer's translation in Pritchard, ed., *Ancient Near Eastern Texts*, pp. 42-44.

3. Leonard Woolley, *Excavations at Ur*, (Thomas Y. Crowell Co., 1965), p. 27.

4. John Bright, "Has Archaeology Found Evidence of the Flood?" *Biblical Archaeologist* 5 (December 1942), pp. 55-62.

5. See, for example, Violet M. Cummings, *Noah's Ark: Fact or Fable?* (Creation-Science Research Center, 1972); John Warwick Montgomery, *The Quest For Noah's Ark* (Minneapolis: Bethany Fellowship, 1974); John D. Morris, *Adventure on Ararat* (San Diego: Institute for Creation Research, 1973); Rene Noorbergen, *The Ark File* (Mountain View, CA: Pacific Press Publishing Assoc., 1974).

6. Fernand Navarra, *Noah's Ark: I Touched It!* (Logos International, 1974), pp. x-xi.

7. See J.C. Whitcomb and H.M. Morris, *The Genesis Flood* (Presbyterian and Reformed Publishers, 1960), pp. 63-79.

8. For a more detailed treatment of these sources, see Speiser, *Genesis* (New York: Doubleday, 1964) or Gerhard Von Rad, *Genesis: A Commentary* (Westminster Press, 1961).

"On the third new moon after the Israelites had gone out of the land of Egypt, on that very day, they came into the wilderness of Sinai. They had journeyed from Rephidim, entered the wilderness of Sinai, and camped in the wilderness; Israel camped there in front of the mountain. Then Moses went up to God; the Lord called to him from the mountain."

(Exodus 19:1-3)

Part III

MT. SINAI

For hundreds of years, pilgrims aspiring to follow in the footsteps of Moses have been ascending the steep cliff Jebel Musa—Arabic for "Mountain of Moses"—in southern Sinai. The stony peak has been associated with the Biblical Mt. Sinai since the fourth century A.D.—but no earlier, leading many scholars to question the identification and encouraging the proposal of alternate sites. In the following chapters, Allen Kerkeslager explores the intriguing possibility—suggested by ancient Jewish sources and modern sleuths—that Mt. Sinai isn't in Sinai at all, but in Arabia. Italian archaeologist Emmanuel Anati, an expert in prehistoric rock art, explains why he believes Har Karkom, in the Negev Desert, provides the most promising parallel to the Biblical Mount Sinai; Israel Finkelstein explains why he disagrees. According to Finkelstein, it's high time archaeologists give up the search.

CHAPTER 3

Mt. Sinai–in Arabia?

Ancient Jewish Tradition Locates Holy Mountain

Allen Kerkeslager

———◦◦◦———

"We set off ... to climb each of the mountains," wrote the fourth-century C.E. Christian pilgrim Egeria of her visit to Mt. Sinai. "They are hard to climb. You do not go round and round them, spiraling up gently, but straight at each one as if you were going up a wall, and then straight down to the foot, till you reach the foot of the central mountain, Sinai itself. Here then, impelled by Christ our God and assisted by the prayers of the holy men who accompanied us, we made the great effort of the climb ... I was not conscious of the effort—in fact I hardly noticed it because, by God's will, I was seeing my hopes coming true."

In the centuries since Egeria toured the Holy Land, many pilgrims have retraced her difficult walk: They travel to St. Catherine's Monastery, which was built by the emperor Justinian as a fortress in the sixth century C.E. at the foot of Jebel Musa, a 7,500-foot peak in the southern Sinai peninsula, and trek before dawn up the jagged granite mountainside. Near the top, they must traverse thousands of steps before they reach the summit. But most find the exertion well worth the effort, for they believe they

Hershel Shanks

The traditional Mt. Sinai—Jebel Musa (the Mountain of Moses)—located in the southern Sinai peninsula has exerted a powerful pull on Christian pilgrims since the fourth century C.E. Travelers seeking to visit the place where Moses is believed to have encountered God begin their 7,500-foot ascent at St. Catherine's Monastery (shown here), at the base of the mountain.

have reached one of the places on earth where the Lord revealed himself to humankind, where the Bible says Moses spent 40 days encountering God and receiving the Ten Commandments, where the Israelites encamped below and demanded that Aaron the high priest fashion a Golden Calf for them, and where an enraged Moses shattered the first Tablets of the Law in response to the Israelites' sin (Exodus 19-20, 32). Later, the prophet Elijah would return to this sacred landscape, hide in a cave and discover God not in the storm, not in the earthquake, not in the fire, but in the still, small voice (1 Kings 19).

But could Egeria and all the pious pilgrims after her have gone to the wrong place? The tradition identifying Jebel Musa as Biblical Mt. Sinai goes back only to the middle of the fourth century C.E. That's a fairly old tradition but still far removed from the eighth to sixth centuries B.C.E., the period in which many scholars believe the Biblical texts describing the revelation at Sinai first coalesced.

The Jebel Musa location for Mt. Sinai is by no means universally accepted. Harvard University professor emeritus Frank Moore Cross, championing a strand of earlier scholarship, has suggested that the real Mt. Sinai is not the mountain that overlooks St. Catherine's.[1] According to Cross and others, it's not even in the Sinai peninsula. They believe Mt. Sinai was in ancient Midian, a region in modern northwestern Saudi Arabia and southern Jordan.

Cross and these other scholars note that Midian played a crucial role in the formation of early Israelite religion. The Bible records that Moses married Zipporah, the daughter of Jethro, a Midianite priest; Jethro advised Moses on setting up courts of law (Exodus 18:13-27). Some scholars have even suggested that Yahweh, the God of the Israelites, was originally a patron deity of the Midianites. Cross finds it telling that the Moses-Midianite connection was retained in tradition despite the fact that the Midianites later became the Israelites' bitter enemies. This makes it quite likely that the Israelite memory of this early Midianite connection is an authentic one. Moreover, intense archaeological surveys in the Sinai peninsula have revealed little from the 13th and 12th centuries B.C.E., the time of the Israelite emergence in

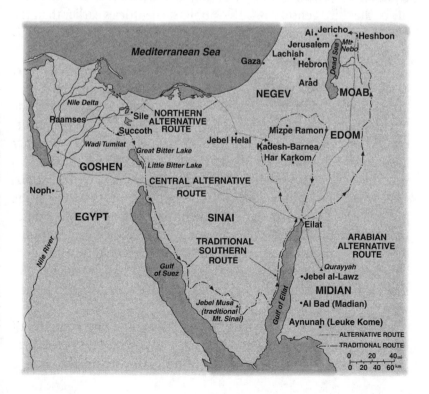

Canaan, while Midian boasted a thriving culture during the same period. A reasonable guess, according to Cross, for the identity of Mt. Sinai is Jebel al-Lawz, the highest peak in northwest Arabia.

Jebel al-Lawz also has the support of two less scholarly, but adventurous, figures, Larry Williams and Bob Cornuke, who managed to sneak onto the mountain in 1988. Williams and Cornuke do not have the archaeological expertise to evaluate properly the materials on the mount, but much of what they found is intriguing and perhaps should not be dismissed out of hand (see the sidebar to this chapter).

With the Saudi government not likely to allow excavation on Jebel al-Lawz any time soon, we cannot learn whether there was an Israelite (or even proto-Israelite) presence in the area in the 13th and 12th centuries B.C.E. But I believe we can learn where some Jews, living during the centuries immediately after the Biblical Mt. Sinai traditions took form, thought the holy mountain was located. The earliest post-Biblical evidence for the location of Mt. Sinai comes from Jewish traditions dating to at least as early as the middle of the third century B.C.E.—about six centuries earlier than the Jebel Musa identification. And the various writings that express this tradition all seem to agree: Mt. Sinai was in Arabia.

The earliest Jewish source, other than the Hebrew Bible, that discusses the location of Mt. Sinai is the Septuagint, the Greek translation of the Hebrew Bible begun in about 250 B.C.E. by the Jewish community in Alexandria, Egypt.[2] The Septuagint transliterates the Hebrew name for Midian into Greek letters as either Madian or Madiam. The translators at times describe the site in a way that suggests they thought of it as a specific city: In Exodus 18:5, where the Hebrew text says that Jethro "came to Moses at the place in the desert where he was camping," the Septuagint states that Jethro, "priest of Madiam," went "out" and then went "into the desert" to meet Moses. Apparently, the Septuagint translators believed that Jethro lived in a city named Madian (Madiam) and that he had to leave the city and go to the desert to meet Moses, who was staying at the foot of Mt. Sinai.

The Septuagint translators seem also to have thought of Madian as a city complete with a city council such as one might find in any Hellenistic city. For example, the Septuagint speaks of the "city (*polis*) of Madiam" as if it had a "council of elders" (*gerousia*) (see its translation of Numbers 22:4,7 and 3 Kingdoms 11:17-18 [=1 Kings 11:17-18 in the Hebrew Bible]).

The Septuagint's occasional use of Madiam for Madian is itself interesting. It can best be explained as the result of the common linguistic phenomenon of euphonic assimilation; in this case, the result of placing the term *polis* (Greek for "city") after the name Madian, in which case the *n* shifts to an *m*, yielding the term *Madiam polis* (a phrase in fact used by Demetrius the Chronographer, an Alexandrian Jew who was a contemporary of the Septuagint translators).

The location of ancient Madian can be determined from a map produced by Ptolemy, a second-century C.E. geographer in Alexandria, and from descriptions of northwestern Arabia in early Islamic literature, which makes frequent references to a city named Madyan.[3] Thanks to these sources, we can confidently identify ancient Madian with a partially excavated site in northwestern Arabia near the modern town of Al-Bad' (also called Mugha'ir Shu'ayb). Qurayyah ware, a pottery style usually associated with the Midianites, indicates that the large oasis at Al-Bad' was probably a Midianite settlement in the Late Bronze and early Iron Ages (13th and 12th centuries B.C.E.). The persistence of the name Madian into the Hellenistic period (332-31 B.C.E.) can be seen as a local remembrance of the earlier Midianite inhabitants.

In the Hellenistic period, Madian sat along the major coastal trade route from Leuke Kome (modern 'Aynunah) to Petra. This route was often traveled by Jewish traders and Jewish mercenaries serving in the Ptolemaic armies in the late fourth and early third centuries B.C.E. Many of these Jews must have made their way beyond this trade route to Alexandria, which was a major cultural center and home to a sizable Jewish community—and where the Septuagint was translated.

Because the Septuagint translators had a specific city in mind when they identified Madian as the hometown of Jethro, and because the account in Exodus of the meeting between Moses and Jethro places Mt. Sinai close to Jethro's home, the Septuagint translators likely believed that Mt. Sinai was a particular mountain not far from the city of Madian.

They were not alone in this belief. In the third century B.C.E., Demetrius the Chronographer claimed that after Moses married Zipporah, the daughter of Jethro, they made their home in the "city of Madiam" (Greek, *Madiam polis*).[4] In fixing the location of the young Moses in the same city mentioned by the Septuagint, Demetrius implicitly agrees with the Septuagint's identification of Mt. Sinai as a mountain near Madian.

Philo, a Jewish philosopher and exegete living in Alexandria in the first half of the first century C.E., gives us another hint as to where Jews in the post-Biblical era thought Mt. Sinai was located. Philo describes Zipporah as an "Arab" who lived in "Arabia."[5] This clearly suggests that, at least in the Alexandrian view of Philo's day, Mt. Sinai was not associated with the Sinai peninsula. The southern Sinai peninsula, which was only beginning to attract the economic interests of the Romans at this time, mattered little to Alexandrians. But the Arabian peninsula mattered greatly: The merchants, dockworkers and shopkeepers of Alexandria profited nicely from the massive trade that passed through their city to and from southern Arabia and India. For them, "Arabia" meant the Arabian peninsula. Precisely the same usage is found in the works of various Alexandrian intellectuals, including the geographers Eratosthenes and Agatharcides.

In addition to his use of the terms "Arab" and "Arabia," Philo gives us an even more direct indication of where he believed Mt. Sinai was. He describes the Israelites wandering eastward all the way across the Sinai peninsula to the southern edge of Palestine just before the revelation at Sinai.[6] Philo thus places Mt. Sinai somewhere east of the Sinai peninsula and south of Palestine—in other words, in northwestern Arabia.

Philo adds one more detail to our collection of traditions about Mt. Sinai; he says that Moses "went up the highest and most sacred of the mountains in its region."[7] Philo's description of the visit of the Israelites to Mt. Sinai has not survived, but given his heavy reliance on the Septuagint in all of his writings, Philo probably agreed with the Septuagint in locating Mt. Sinai near the city of Madian.[8] Since Philo believed that Mt. Sinai was the highest mountain in the region, he must have believed that it was the highest mountain near Madian.

Did Amateur Archaeologists Find the Real Mt. Sinai?

In 1988 Wall Street millionaire Larry Williams and ex-cop Bob Cornuke snuck into Saudi Arabia on a mission to explore what they believed was the real Mt. Sinai—Jebel al-Lawz. Using the Book of Exodus as their guide, they searched the 8,500-foot-high peak for evidence that this was the site where Moses received the Ten Commandments.

Williams and Cornuke were following in the footsteps of the self-proclaimed archaeologists Ron Wyatt and David Fasold, who visited the mountain in 1986 hoping to find the "gold of Exodus"—the Egyptian jewelry that they believed the Israelites had brought with them from Egypt (Exodus 12:35-36). Wyatt and Fasold did not get far: After only one morning on the mountain, they were arrested for illegal excavation, threatened with capital punishment and deported.

Knowing of Larry Williams's interest in Biblical finds, Fasold informed the millionaire of their curtailed excavations and told him that his metal detector

had indicated that the plains around Jebel al-Lawz were rich with buried gold. Enticed, Williams in turn contacted Cornuke, a former policeman with a reputation for bravery. Together, they decided to enter Saudi Arabia illegally and explore Mt. Sinai. The story of their clandestine trip to Jebel al-Lawz has been recounted in videos and books—including the *New York Times* bestseller *The Gold of Exodus*, by Howard Blum.

Like others before them, Williams and Cornuke identify Jebel al-Lawz as Mt. Sinai primarily because it is the highest mountain in what some scholars identify as the ancient region of Midian. They also note that the summit is black and appears to be composed of charred rock, recalling the description in Exodus: "Mount Sinai was wrapped in smoke, because the Lord had descended upon it in fire; the smoke went up like the smoke of a kiln" (Exodus 19:18). Further, the vast open space surrounding the mountain, they suggest, would have supported the multitude of Israelites, and a nearby plain could have served as the battleground of Rephidim (Exodus 17:8-13).

Poking around the fenced-off site, Williams and Cornuke searched for further correspondences with the Biblical record. Near the foot of the mountain, they spotted a stack of boulders bearing petroglyphs (rock drawings) of bulls: This, Williams and Cornuke suggest, might be the altar where the Israelites worshiped the golden calf (photo, p. 39). Also around the base of the mountain, the pair found a long line of widely spaced rock piles, or cairns, that they suggest may be the boundary markers erected by Moses around the base of Mt. Sinai: "The Lord said to Moses, '... You shall set bounds for the people round about, saying, "Beware of going up the mountain or touching the border of it"'" (Exodus 19:10-12).

Higher up the slope, Cornuke and Williams found a large stone structure resembling the foundation of a building with two wings (each 30 by 65 feet) meeting at right angles. Right next to the structure they discovered the remnants of marble columns, and not too far away Cornuke and Williams found the remains of what they identify as 12 large stone towers, each about 18 feet in diameter. They tentatively identify the foundation with the altar constructed by Moses in Exodus 24; the towers with the 12 pillars Moses erected: "Moses built an altar ... and set up twelve stones representing the twelve tribes of Israel" (Exodus 24:4). The columns, they suggest, might be the remains of a much later temple.

In the cloak of darkness, Cornuke and Williams scaled the mountain. Near the upper reaches, they detected a cleft in the rock. Could this be where God revealed himself to Moses, they speculated? "As my Presence passes by," God told Moses, "I will put you in a cleft of the rock and shield you with My hand until I have passed by" (Exodus 33:21-22). They also found a large cave on the side of the mountain, which they suggest may have been the cave of Elijah (1 Kings 19:8-13).

But there is little real evidence to support their identifications. According to Allen Kerkeslager, author of the accompanying article, cattle are prominent in the rock art found around Jebel al-Lawz, but they also appear in a wide variety of locations in northwestern Arabia. "In some cases the petroglyphs of cattle in this region may indeed have had a ritual function," Kerkeslager says. "But in other cases they were intended simply to communicate messages about hunting, pastoral activity or some other relatively mundane concerns."

The marble columns near the building foundation could be the work of the Nabateans, who lived in the area from the second century B.C.E. to the second century C.E. and who used similar columns in their temples. The proximity of the columns to the stone foundation might indicate that this structure, too, dates to the later period. Further, the 12 towers, according to Kerkeslager, are similar to tumuli (stone mounds) found throughout northwest Arabia. Some of the earliest excavated examples are funerary markers from the Neolithic period (8300-4800 B.C.E.). The 12 tumuli at Jebel al-Lawz might come from the traditional period of Moses, but they might also predate him by more than 3,000 years. The stone cairns that Williams and Cornuke identified as Israelite boundary markers are also common throughout northwest Arabia and can date anywhere from the Paleolithic era (before 8300 B.C.E.) to the Roman period (after the first century B.C.E.). But, as Kerkeslager notes, none of this material can be evaluated properly without a record of the pottery associated with it.

Williams and Cornuke are not archaeologists. As they readily admit, they do not know how to look for or interpret the sort of evidence that would reveal the archaeological context of Jebel al-Lawz. As Kerkeslager notes, they have produced no scientific evidence that furthers our understanding of the site's relation to the period of the Exodus. Nevertheless, their midnight exploration has piqued popular interest. Whether their identification is accurate or not, might some of the elements they observed—the height of the mountain, the blackened top, the cleft in the rock, the rock art—have inspired ancient visitors to identify this mountain as Mt. Sinai? We can only hope that their illicit excursion will lead to further excavation by archaeologists working with—rather than against—Saudi authorities.

The earliest post-Biblical Jewish sources from Palestine indicate that Jews there shared the view of those in Alexandria regarding the location of Mt. Sinai. The mid-second-century B.C.E. Book of Jubilees, fragments of which were found among the Dead Sea Scrolls, gives a long and idealized description of world geography that seems to suggest the author believed Mt. Sinai was in the Arabian peninsula (Jubilees 8:19).[9]

The apostle Paul also seems to have located Mt. Sinai in Arabia. New Testament scholar Jerome Murphy-O'Connor and others have argued that Paul's mention of a sojourn in Arabia in Galatians 1:16-17 is actually a reference to Paul's missionary activity among the Nabateans, who lived southeast of the Dead Sea.[10] But this is based largely on inferences from Paul's later missionary activity. Since this visit to Arabia was followed by three years in Damascus (Galatians 1:18), no time is left in the chronology of Paul's life (as known from other sources) for a long period of missionary activity in Arabia. The grammatical structure of Galatians 1:15-18 demands a rather different interpretation, such as the following paraphrase: "When God … was pleased to reveal his son in me … I did not immediately consult with flesh and blood, and I did not go up to Jerusalem to those who were apostles before me (to consult with them), but I went away into Arabia (to consult with God) and again returned to Damascus." Paul, like many other Jews in this period, may have briefly gone into the desert to acquire revelation in conscious imitation of Moses and Elijah. The odd choice of Arabia for this quest is best explained if Paul actually went to Mt. Sinai itself. This might be confirmed by Galatians 4:25, where either Paul or a later copyist in the Pauline tradition added a parenthesis that reads (in the best manuscripts) "Sinai is a mountain in Arabia."

The clearest description in early Jewish literature of the location of Mt. Sinai comes from the first-century C.E. Jewish historian Flavius Josephus. He places Rephidim, the station of the Exodus where the Israelites encamped just before their arrival at Sinai, in the region of the Nabatean city of Petra.[11] This would have put the Israelites directly west of Mt. Seir, which is in modern southwestern Jordan. With Mt. Seir to the east, and not wanting to head west back towards Egypt, the

Israelites would have had to choose between going north or south. But going north would have brought them to Palestine, so they turned south—towards northwest Arabia. With no other stops between Rephidim and Mt. Sinai, the sacred mountain could not have been far south into the Arabian peninsula.

Indeed, Josephus writes that Mt. Sinai was "the highest of the mountains" in the region of "the city of Madiane."[12] So Josephus, too, seconds the testimony of the Septuagint and other Jewish writers from the Hellenistic and Roman periods regarding the location of Mt. Sinai.

Given the early Christian use of the Septuagint and the works of Jewish authors writing in Greek, it is not surprising that the Jewish tradition of locating Mt. Sinai near the city of Madian in northwest Arabia was picked up by such early church fathers (mid-third to early fifth century C.E.) as Origen,[13] Eusebius[14] and Jerome.[15] The tradition also seems to have survived in monastic circles in ancient Madian until the Arab conquest in the seventh century C.E., after which it makes its first appearance in Islamic literature. By about 900 C.E., Madian had become identified in Islamic tradition with the home of Jethro, the father-in-law of Moses.[16] At about the same time, Jethro became identified with the pre-Islamic prophet Shu'ayb, whose name is preserved in the local name given to Al-Bad' (ancient Madian), Mugha'ir Shu'ayb.

So where does this leave Jebel al-Lawz?

The peak was easily visible to ancient Jewish travelers passing along the route from Leuke Kome to Petra. In the oddly blackened top of the mountain, some Jews may have found testimony to the burning fire and cloud of smoke that Exodus 19:18 says rested on Mt. Sinai when the Law was given. Jebel al-Lawz is only 20 miles from ancient Madian, so it is certainly a good candidate for a northwest Arabian Mt. Sinai. Even more in its favor is the fact that at 8,500 feet it is the highest peak in the area.

But we must caution against relying too heavily on these post-Biblical Jewish traditions in identifying Mt. Sinai. We do not know the sources of these traditions or how accurate they are. Some Jews in the Hellenistic and Roman eras, including Paul,

Jebel al-Lawz is the tallest mountain in ancient Madian, the western Arabian region where several ancient Jewish sources locate Mt. Sinai. Recently, amateur explorers have suggested that its oddly blackened top (photo at top) is an indication that this is the site where God, amid fire and smoke, revealed the Law to Moses.

may well have made pilgrimages to what they believed was Mt. Sinai in hopes of gaining revelation, just as Moses and Elijah had (see Galatians 1:17).[17] But the mountain they chose may not have been the same one that the early editors of the Hebrew Bible had in mind. Like many other conjectures made by early interpreters of the Hebrew Bible, speculation about the site of Mt. Sinai may simply have been wrong.

Even if this Jewish tradition is right and Mt. Sinai is indeed in northwest Arabia, Jebel al-Lawz may not be the right mountain. The tradition that Mt. Sinai was the highest mountain near Madian may seem to point to Jebel al-Lawz because it is clearly the peak that dominates the entire region. But a mountain closer to Madian may also have been meant.

Madian is located in a large oasis in the heart of ancient Midian. Jebel al-Lawz looms nearby. A modern archaeological expedition to the mountain would no doubt uncover much valuable information, though current research suggests that a large segment of the early Israelites were indigenous Canaanites, so we should not expect to find a lot of evidence for the events described in Exodus. Even more valuable, to my mind, would be an excavation of Madian itself. This ancient site, long thought by Jews, Christians and Muslims to have been the setting for some of the Bible's most dramatic events, might well yield important insights into the cultural context of Israelite origins.[18]

1. See "Frank Moore Cross, An Interview, Part I: Israelite Origins," *Bible Review*, August 1992.

2. See Leonard Greenspoon, "Mission to Alexandria: Truth and Legend About the Creation of the Septuagint, the First Bible Translation," *Bible Review*, August 1989.

3. See Allen Kerkeslager, "Jewish Pilgrimage and Jewish Identity in Hellenistic and Early Roman Egypt," in *Pilgrimage and Holy Space in Late Antique Egypt*, ed. David Frankfurter, *Religions in the Graeco-Roman World* 134 (Leiden: Brill, 1998), pp. 156-158, 199-200.

4. Cited in Eusebius, *Praeparatio Evangelica* 9.29.1-3.

5. Philo, *On the Life of Moses* 1.47, 51-52; cf. *On the Virtues* 34; *On the Life of Joseph* 15.

6. Philo, *Moses* 1.163-220; cf. Exodus 17:8-16, 19:1-2.

7. Philo, *Moses* 2.70.

8. Philo, *Allegorical Interpretation* 12-13; *Agriculture* 43; *On the Confusion of Tongues* 55-57; *On the Change of Names* 106-120.

9. See Kerkeslager, "Jewish Pilgrimage," pp. 169-175.

10. For a contrasting view of Paul's use of the term "Arabia," see Jerome Murphy-O'Connor, "What Was Paul Doing in 'Arabia'?" *Bible Review*, October 1994.

11. Josephus, *Antiquities of the Jews* 3.33,39-40,62.

12. Josephus, *Antiquities* 2.257,264-265, 3.76.

13. Origen, *Selecta in Genesim* 39, in *Patrologia Graeca* 12.120.

14. Eusebius, *Onomasticon* 124, 172.

15. See Jerome's Latin translation of Eusebius, *Onomasticon* 125, 143, 167 and 172-173.

16. F. Buhl and C.E. Bosworth, "Madyan Shu'ayb," in *Encyclopedia of Islam*, ed. C.E. Bosworth et al. (Leiden: Brill, 1986), vol. 5, pp. 1155-1156; Alois Musil, *The Northern Hegaz: A Topographical Itinerary* (New York: American Geographical Society, 1926), pp. 109-118, 278-282.

17. This might also have been true of the Jewish author of the Apocalypse of Abraham (see 12:1-3).

18. The author would like to thank Robert Cornuke for kindly supplying photographs and helpful information for this article.

CHAPTER 4

Mt. Sinai–in the Negev?

Ancient Cult Center Discovered on Desert Peak

Emmanuel Anati

———⋙⋘———

I first came upon the mountain in 1955, when I was conducting an archaeological survey in the Negev on behalf of the Israel Department of Antiquities (now called the Israel Antiquities Authority). At the time, I knew the mountain as Jebel Ideid. That is what the Bedouin called it. It was located in Israel just 4 miles from the border with Egypt, about 65 miles south of my field base at the young kibbutz of Sde Boker, where David Ben Gurion, Israel's first Prime Minister, then lived.

I was there because of my interest in the virtually unknown rock art of the area—figures and signs engraved by ancient people on rocks.[1] On this particular mountain, located between the huge gorge known as the Machtesh Ramon and the Aravah Valley, which extends from the Dead Sea to the Gulf of Eila, I found the richest concentration of rock art ever discovered in the Negev.

While some of the styles and groups of rock engravings were similar to those I had found in the central Negev, others were quite different. Some assemblages, with which I was familiar, belonged to what is known today as Period III of rock art, the Chalcolithic Age

Har Karkom emerges abruptly from the sands of the Negev Desert near today's border between Israel and Egypt. On this imposing mountain, 2,795 feet above sea level, author Emmanuel Anati discovered an unusual ancient cult site, with standing stones, altars, temples, encampments and the greatest concentration of rock art ever discovered in the Negev.

(fourth millennium B.C.). These engravings included beautiful hunting scenes in which the hunters wore skin garments, used a bow and arrow, and were assisted by dogs. Other assemblages were also of a familiar character, showing a style known as Period IV-C, usually connected with the Nabateans near the turn of the era, and still others were inscriptions from Hellenistic and Roman times.

Between these two assemblages was another category of art that was strange to me. It turned out to be a local version of the Bronze Age art known as Period IV-A (dating mainly to the third millennium B.C.). The assemblages at Jebel Ideid included depictions of worshipers standing before strange abstract symbols. For example, one scene, repeated several times, shows a praying man with upraised hands standing before a simple line.

From this same period, we also found some *menhirs*, or standing stone pillars. *Menhir*, an archaeological term, is the Breton word for standing stone; in the Bible such *menhirs* are known as *masseboth* (singular, *massebah*). Other discoveries included a peculiar stone structure with a courtyard and a rectangular platform facing east. Several tumuli (piles of stones that usually cover tombs) were also located on the mountain. One of these tumuli had a flat stone on top; beneath this stone was a large piece of a jar decorated in what is known as "metallic ware" that enabled us to date the tumulus to about 2000 B.C.

The mountain overlooks the Wadi Djirafi, in the area that Israeli geographical maps call the Desert of Paran. Hundreds of canyons wind through the hills of the desert. A traveler can go for miles without seeing a blade of grass. Ultimately, all the canyons, or wadis (dry riverbeds subject to periodic flooding), converge on the great wadi known as the Aravah, which extends south from the Dead Sea to the Gulf of Eilat. It is a barren, powerful and essential land.

Emmanuel Anati

Dated to the third millennium B.C., this rock engraving at Har Karkom depicts a stick-like male figure praying before a simple vertical line.

The first time I climbed Jebel Ideid, in 1955, I was struck by the vastness of the view from the top. Looking to the south and to the east, I felt as if I could almost hold in my hand the broken landscape going down to the Aravah and beyond to the distant hazy profile of the mountains of Moab and Edom on the other side of the great rift, in what is now Jordan. To the west, the panorama encompassed the slopes and hills of central Sinai, crossed for thousands of years by caravans traveling between Arabia and the Mediterranean Sea on the spice route known as the Darb el-Aza. To the north I could see the mountains and valleys leading to the central Negev, and the watershed of the Machtesh Ramon.

In all this surrounding immense landscape, I could see no sign of human life. The mountain on which I stood dominated an endless desert, an empty quarter of the world. We knew of no other archaeological remains or rock art for miles around the mountain. The absolute silence was broken only by what sounded like a prolonged explosion—a mass of large boulders becoming detached from the wall of a precipice and falling into the valley.

Yet on the mountain itself and the areas leading up to it, the remains of human activity abound. Why here? And what did all these indications of ancient human activity mean? Unfortunately, the first time I climbed the mountain I was able to spend only one day. I had no answers for my many questions. But I knew that some day I would return.

In the 1970s, as head of the Italian archaeological expedition to the Near East sponsored by the Centro Camuno di Studi Preistorici, I decided to return to Jebel Ideid to study its archaeological remains more thoroughly and perhaps to answer some of the questions that had intrigued me years before. Strangely enough, I could not locate the mountain. Several attempts failed. The few Bedouin I had known in the area 20 years before had since moved on; there was no one left to point out the route. New and more detailed geographical maps of the area had been made by the Israelis, but the name of this mountain, like many others, had changed. The new names no longer corresponded to those given to me by my Bedouin guides in the 1950s. And after 20 years, although I remembered the impact that the place had had on me, the landscape, the very atmosphere and the rock art I had photographed and published, I could not recall details of the paths leading to the mountain. My staff and I tried repeatedly to find Jebel Ideid, but failed. It seemed simply to have disappeared.

Then, in 1980, 25 years after my previous visit, quite by accident, it was suddenly relocated.

Since then I have returned to the site many times—and archaeological expeditions continue today[2]—but certainly nothing will ever equal the thrill of our rediscovery of the site in 1980.

The only easy access to the mountain was through a large valley to the west, which can be reached only through a mountain pass that was very difficult to find until a trail had been clearly defined. There is now a jeep trail to the site, and during our field season we have direct communications with Mizpe Ramon, the nearest permanent settlement some 62 miles away. On the new Israeli maps, the site is called Har Karkom, Mount Saffron in English. Henceforth we will refer to it as Har Karkom.

Strangely enough, despite the extreme elusiveness of the mountain, Har Karkom dominates the land around it, known as the Desert of Paran. It is visible from over 47 miles away, from the mountains of Edom in Jordan. Vertically, Har Karkom has a rectangular outline that imposes itself on the horizon and makes it an obvious point of reference for travelers crossing the desert even today, as it must have done for travelers in the past. Had we noticed this when we first found the mountain in 1955, we would have been spared a great deal of effort in relocating it.

For the most part, the trail to the western valley is relatively easy, although there is one difficult pass that must be negotiated with effort and care. Then the ground becomes extremely rough and uneven and cracked by erosion for a few miles.

The mountain itself consists of a limestone plateau (I shall refer to this plateau frequently) with outcrops of flint. It is quite large, measuring over 2.5 miles from north to south, and averaging 1.2 miles from east to west. Its maximum height is 2,795 feet above sea level, and it is almost completely surrounded by steep precipices.

On the plateau are two hills that rise 230 feet above the plateau. From the west they appear like the breasts of a large woman. Depressions and small valleys cover the rest of the plateau and descend toward the ravines to the west and southwest.

Har Karkom can be approached most easily from the west because the precipices on the other sides are in most places too sheer to climb. On the west side, there are, in fact, two well-worn paths with some surprising features. One was partially cut by man at one point to facilitate the climb. Along the way are small caves that reveal distinct evidence of human presence and use.

The other path is even more unusual: On either side of it, for about a mile, are small rocks decorated with engravings. Many of them portray scenes of adoration—figures in the conventional praying position with upraised arms, before hermetic signs— signs clear only to those who have the key to understand them. In each of at least four cases, the praying figure stands before a vertical line. The scene appears to depict the worship of an abstract, unrepresentable deity.

Along this path are also several orthostats, or *menhirs*, oblong standing stones intentionally set in vertical positions. Placed midway along the path is a *menhir* with two smaller stones, at its base, engraved with figures. This grouping recalls a religious practice mentioned in the Bible: "And this stone which I have set for a pillar (*massebah*), shall be God's house" (Genesis 28:22).

This winding path that leads towards the plateau resembles a kind of prehistoric *Via Crucis*, with stopping stations at which people carved the rocks with praying figures, erected *masseboth*, and perhaps performed other rites of worship as well.

At the foot of the mountain, where the two paths begin, is the western valley. Here our expedition set up its camp. Close by are vestiges of ancient walls and stone foundations, representing the encampments of peoples who stayed in this area ages ago. Above the valley rises the sphinx-like silhouette of the mountain, which our expedition climbed daily during our periods of fieldwork.

This mountain and its immediate surroundings have revealed to date over 400 archaeological sites—all in the midst of a wasteland where our quite thorough surveys have uncovered very few archaeological remains.

The exceptionally large number of archaeological finds associated with the mountain, the types of rock art and monuments, indicate that Har Karkom must have been a sacred mountain in ancient times, a place of worship of tremendous importance.

The wealth of rock art is extraordinary. On several clusters of rocky outcrops, we counted hundreds of engraved figures. All told, there are well over 35,000 engraved figures on Har Karkom. It is thus the greatest concentration of rock art known to us in the entire Negev.

The figures are executed in styles and techniques well known elsewhere in the Middle East. As a result of our research, we have developed a chronology of rock art in the Negev and Sinai based on stylistic characteristics.

From the information on the distribution of rock art styles at Har Karkom, we can roughly trace the history of human activity at the site, even though there is considerable overlap in the periods assigned to each category.

The practice of engraving rocks started in this area in the Neolithic period (eighth to fifth millennium B.C.), but it became widespread in the late Chalcolithic period (fourth millennium B.C.). The greatest creative activity is in style Period IV-A (58 sites), which dates to what archaeologists call the Early Bronze

Age and Middle Bronze Age I (roughly, the third millennium B.C.). Several thousand figures belong to this period.

Then there is nothing until the Hellenistic period (332 to 37 B.C.). This gap (starting during Period IV-B) is extremely significant. It lasts for roughly 1,600 years.

The same pattern is repeated when we focus on the archaeological remains instead of the rock art, with one major exception: Although the Paleolithic period (80,000 to 10,000 B.C.) is not represented by any rock art, we did find a large number of virtually intact Paleolithic sites right on the surface of the plateau.

The remains of Paleolithic foundations of huts actually delineate the plan of the encampments. These huts are primarily oval-shaped. The inhabitants had cleared the huts of stones, which they then placed around the outer perimeter of the encampment, no doubt to hold down the animal skins or other perishable material used as roofs for the structures.

Within the encampment, we found flint-cutting workshops, with flint cores and the flint flakes that had been removed from them lying *in situ*, just as they had been left tens of thousands of years ago. The flint is of excellent quality; the large number of flint workshops suggests that this raw material may have attracted Paleolithic people to the mountain.

The finds from a single encampment, about 40 by 45 meters in size and consisting of eight huts, gives an idea of the amount of flint worked here. Within an area of 108 square feet on the edge of the settlement, we collected over 110 pounds of fine, elegant flint implements.

The archaeological evidence indicates that from the ninth to the fifth millennium B.C., there was very little activity on the mountain. Of all the sites, only one yielded evidence of the presence of people during this period.

This changes toward the end of the Chalcolithic period (latter part of the fourth millennium B.C.) and especially during the Early Bronze Age (third millennium B.C.), when the archaeological evidence suggests considerable activity at the mountain. On the plateau itself we found numerous remains of funerary and religious structures, as well as groups of tumuli and circles of boulders, which often enclosed standing stones (*menhirs*, or *masseboth*). Some of the rocks were engraved with decorations and figures. We excavated one of these tumuli and found a bundle of human long bones, a clear sign of secondary burial. The only object buried with these remains was a perforated shell-disk pendant.

We also discovered three larger stone structures from the Early Bronze Age. Each of these rather curious structures has a round courtyard in front of it. On one side of each courtyard is an altar-like platform. Two of these structures were found at the foot of the mountain in the western valley. The third is located in the center of the plateau, where it commands a beautiful view of the entire surrounding area. On the eastern side of each of these stone structures, we found a number of *masseboth*. *Masseboth* were also found in front of and beside the altar-like platforms. On the far side of each courtyard was a small room, probably the only part of the structure that might have been covered by a roof. Rock engravings and funerary tumuli surround the structures. The nature and setting of these buildings seem to indicate that they were small temples.

In the valley at the foot of the mountain, where the two trails to the top begin, we found traces of at least ten major encampments from the same period. We also noted several small lateral settlements, as well as one much larger central one (called Site No. 50) that contained the remains of more than 50 groups of structures. Other camping sites were found for some 4.5 miles along the wadi northwest of the mountain. Apparently, a considerable number of people once lived at the foot of the mountain. On the mountain itself there are numerous Bronze Age sites of worship, and new camping sites are situated in the valleys at its base. Significantly, these extensive remains are located in a desert area where, at least today, there is no trace of any oasis.

The artifacts from the sites of this period include both pottery and stone implements. Worked flint implements are characteristic of the Chalcolithic and the Early Bronze Ages; among those we found were blunt back-blades; several types of scrapers, including fan scrapers; notched implements and various kinds of pointed blades. We also found many retooled flint implements that were originally made in the Paleolithic period but were reworked and reused in the late Chalcolithic period or the Bronze Age. In fact, one of the recurring characteristics of these assemblages is the reuse of older implements. The lighter patina where the flint was retouched reveals the secondary use.

The majority of the pottery consists of minuscule sherds that have been dated mainly by Israeli archaeologists, led by Rudolph Cohen, the former district archaeologist for the Negev. Cohen's team of experts dated the pottery to the Early Bronze Age II (2900-2600 B.C.) and the Middle Bronze Age I (2200-2000 B.C.). For both assemblages, the most common shape of pot is a hole-mouth jar with a flat base.

The dwelling structures seem to be characteristic of seminomadic, semipermanent populations. The houses had been reused more than once over the years. At several sites, pottery defined as belonging to the Early Bronze Age was found in the very same courtyards and rooms as pottery from the Middle Bronze Age I. Although pottery experts propose precise dates for these finds, one cannot exclude the possibility that in this area there was a direct cultural continuity between the Early Bronze II and Middle Bronze I period, as Rudolph Cohen suggested two years ago.[3]

This Bronze Age complex undoubtedly reflects a tribal way of life, of communities living in marginal or peripheral areas. The organization of the sites indicates that these seminomadic, or semisedentary, people consisted of tribes organized in large family groups over a long period of time. The Chalcolithic flints suggest that this tradition goes back to the fourth millennium B.C. Most of it, however, can safely be attributed to the third millennium B.C.

The populations that lived in marginal areas like this must have been able to maintain their own traditions, almost completely uninfluenced by the agricultural and military upheavals that occurred in the fertile areas of Syria-Palestine. It is perhaps significant that this mountain must have been an extremely important source of prime-quality flint in Paleolithic times. It appears to have become a holy place at the very end of the Stone Age, at a time when the use of flint as the material of primary daily use was drawing to a close. However, flint continued to be used extensively in the Early Bronze Age, and the quantity of very large and refined tools hints at its ritual use.

It appears, therefore, that Har Karkom was intensely occupied during the Paleolithic Age by hunting clans that collected and worked fine-quality flint in the area. The area was virtually abandoned in the Neolithic period; we found only one site from this period. Then, beginning in the late Chalcolithic or the Early Bronze Age, there was a period of intense occupation, reflected in the numerous religious and burial sites on the mountain and the dwelling encampments at its base. This period lasted for about a thousand years. During this time, the mountain was a place of worship, of pilgrimages, of religious rites and of funerary activities. After the Middle Bronze I period, the site was again virtually abandoned—for the entire second millennium and for most of the first millennium—until the Nabateans occupied the region.

It was clear from the very beginning of our survey that Har Karkom was an important cult center in the third millennium B.C., a kind of prehistoric Mecca where large groups of people came and built their camps at the foothills and then climbed the plateau to worship. *Menhirs*, stone circles, tumuli, altar-like structures, peculiar round platforms with "altars" on top of them were all clear indications of religious activities. Add to this the enormous amount of religious rock art and the remains of three small temples, and there can be no doubt that Har Karkom presents a unique aggregation of evidence of religious activity during the Bronze Age Complex. Har Karkom remained a great center of worship for at least a millennium before it was abandoned around 2000 B.C. We know of no other site like it in the Negev or Sinai.

Might this unusual center of worship, located on a desert mountain, be related to the Biblical Mt. Sinai?

Although Har Karkom's religious character was quite evident, I made no connection between that mountain and Mt. Sinai for several years. As an archaeologist, not a Biblical scholar, I never questioned that the Exodus had occurred in about the 13th century B.C. and that this was a firmly established fact. I had learned this date at school, from my textbooks, and had no reason to think otherwise.

There was no evidence of any human occupation at Har Karkom in the 13th century B.C. or for centuries before or after. Indeed, the usual date for the Exodus occurred right in the middle of a long archaeological gap at Har Karkom.

Another factor that at first excluded any consideration of a relationship between Har Karkom and the Exodus was the location of the site, far from any previously proposed itinerary of the Exodus. Some scholars viewed the wanderings of the children of Israel in the desert as random movements from one well to another. Others saw it as consisting of an itinerary from Egypt south to the traditional Mt. Sinai located in the southern part of the peninsula, and from there to Ein el-Qudeirat, which is believed to be Kadesh-Barnea. Still others suggested the possibility that the Exodus itinerary described sites along the Mediterranean coast of northern Sinai. There are several other hypotheses, none of which include our area.

Nevertheless, we thought it possible that such an important cult site as we had found on the edge of the Holy Land would be referred to in the Bible, if we could only figure out by what name. As archaeologists, however, this was not our primary concern.

I did, however, consult several colleagues who were Biblical scholars. I always received the same answer: The finds at Har Karkom were too early to have a Biblical connection. One of the greatest living Biblical scholars twitted me for exaggerating the significance of Har Karkom. The whole Sinai peninsula and the Negev were probably full of holy mountains, he told me, so we should not be bothered trying to find references to Har Karkom in the Bible. To this I reacted very strongly; there was something wrong in this approach. I knew Sinai and the Negev very well. I had worked there for 30 years. I had never seen another mountain with such vast evidence of worship and of tribal gatherings as Har Karkom. It was hard for me to believe that such a site would not be mentioned in the Bible.

On the last day of our 1982 campaign—December 20 to be exact—I was climbing down the mountain as the sun was descending in the western sky. Every stone was etched in sharp shadows. Suddenly, I saw the silhouette of a strange sequence of standing stones beside one of the archaeological sites near our camp. Although I had visited this particular site several times before, I had never noticed it in this light. The members of our expedition were packing and I made a short detour to examine more closely this structure at the edge of one of the Bronze Age camp sites (Site No. 52) at the foot of the mountain. There was a group of 12 pillars or standing stones fixed vertically into the ground. Next to this group of *masseboth* were the remains of a structure that could not have been a dwelling place—it contained a platform and a courtyard. The surface finds did not indicate that it included any roofed rooms. This group of 12 pillars and the platform nearby vaguely reminded me of a passage in the Bible. I went on to our camp and took out a Bible and found the passage: "And Moses ... rose up early in the morning, and built an altar under the hill, and 12 pillars, according to the 12 tribes of Israel" (Exodus 24:4). Twelve is a recurring number in the Bible; it is, nevertheless, surprising that 12 pillars and a nearby structure were found "under" (at the foot of) the "hill" (or mountain), at the edge of the camp site.

Archaeologists examine 12 standing stones erected next to what may have been an altar. This configuration, Anati suggests, could be the "altar under the hill, and 12 pillars, according to the 12 tribes of Israel," that Moses set up on Mt. Sinai (Exodus 24:4).

I asked some members of my team to go to Site No. 52 with me and, standing there, I read them the passage from the Bible. We had a long discussion, and two additional items of interest came up, one relating to a cleft in the rock on the top of the mountain and the other to the small temple on the plateau of the mountain.

The cleft on the top of the mountain forms a small rock shelter that bears a striking correspondence to the cleft in the rock on the top of Mt. Sinai described in Exodus 33:21-22: "And the Lord said, Behold, there is a place by me, and you shall stand upon a rock; And it shall come to pass, while my glory passes by, that I will put you in the cleft of the rock, and will cover you with my hand while I pass by." To find such a niche or cleft on the very summit of a mountain is geologically quite unusual. I know of only one other such cleft on the top of a mountain: the cave on Jerusalem's Temple Mount, which is the traditional Mount Moriah, another very important holy place of Biblical times. On Mount Moriah, according to the Bible, Abraham offered to sacrifice his only son Isaac. Today the Dome of the Rock stands on this site sanctified by tradition.

The second item of interest that was raised in our discussion was the small Bronze Age temple at the center of the plateau of the mountain. In the courtyard of the temple was an elevated platform oriented toward the east. Surrounding the little temple were various funerary tumuli and rock engravings, as well as numerous carvings of footprints; those carvings are now known to be connected with worship. The Bible seems to make clear that Moses saw an old temple on Mt. Sinai, which he later used as a model and prototype: "And look that they make them after their pattern, which was showed you on the mountain" (Exodus 25:40). And "hollow with boards shall you make it [the altar]; as it was showed you on the mountain, so shall they make it" (Exodus 27:8). The only area of this little sanctuary that seems to have been roofed was a small room, about 10 by 13 feet, with stone walls that originally must have been about 5 feet high. The roof was probably made of animal skins or some other perishable material. As the Bible describes it: "And you shall make curtains of goats' hair to be a covering upon the tabernacle; eleven curtains shall thou make" (Exodus 26:7). And further on: "And you shall rear up the tabernacle according to the fashion thereof which was showed you on the mountain" (Exodus 26:30). Some Biblical scholars believe that Moses may have had a vision of a "celestial" temple while on the mountain. Could it be possible instead that an ancient temple stood on the mountain that the Bible describes as Sinai?

Among the cult sites on the plateau of Har Karkom are numerous funerary tumuli. They suggest a specific burial custom in which the bones of the dead were preserved and eventually brought to be buried on such hallowed ground as this mountaintop. The Bible describes a similar practice, when the Israelites fleeing from Egypt carried the bones of Joseph with them: "And Moses took the bones of Joseph with him: for he had straightly sworn the children of Israel, saying, 'God will surely visit you; and you shall carry my bones with you from here'" (Exodus 13:19). Archaeological finds have shown that secondary burial under tumuli was practiced by Early Bronze Age cultures, but the practice came to an end at the beginning of the Middle Bronze Age.

The rock engravings so abundantly represented at Har Karkom provide another intriguing comparison. As mentioned already, much of the rock art at Har Karkom can be dated to the Bronze Age. Many of these engravings contain occult signs that are incomprehensible to us now, but that must have had a specific significance for the people who executed them. In some cases, these engravings include series of parallel lines, or points, often eight or ten, perhaps indicating points to remember or memorize. Today, one might say, "Tie ten knots in your handkerchief." In one case, we even found an engraving of a rectangular stone tablet with two ear-like shapes on top. Lines divided the tablet into ten squares.

The Bible is not explicit as to what was engraved on the tablets containing the Ten Commandments. We are told that the two stones were later preserved in the Temple at Jerusalem. But nowhere are we told whether they were engraved with a script, either ancient Semitic or Egyptian, or with symbols or with simple markings. Any script would probably have been unintelligible to the majority of the Israelites fleeing from Egyptian slavery. It is quite conceivable that the Tablets of the Law were actually slabs of rocks engraved with symbols or markings not unlike those found along the paths and on the plateau of Har Karkom.

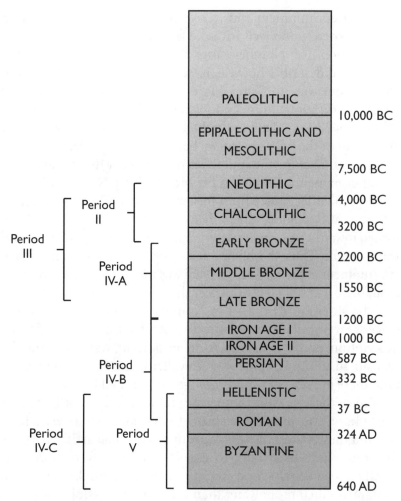

	PALEOLITHIC	
		10,000 BC
	EPIPALEOLITHIC AND MESOLITHIC	
		7,500 BC
Period II	NEOLITHIC	4,000 BC
	CHALCOLITHIC	3200 BC
Period III	EARLY BRONZE	2200 BC
Period IV-A	MIDDLE BRONZE	1550 BC
	LATE BRONZE	1200 BC
	IRON AGE I	1000 BC
Period IV-B	IRON AGE II	587 BC
	PERSIAN	332 BC
Period IV-C / Period V	HELLENISTIC	37 BC
	ROMAN	324 AD
	BYZANTINE	640 AD

There are other aspects in which Har Karkom evokes Biblical descriptions of the Sinai event. For example, consider this description of the Israelite encampment at the foot of Mt. Sinai: "On the third new moon after the Israelites had gone out of the land of Egypt, on that very day, they came into the wilderness of Sinai. They had journeyed from Rephidim, entered the wilderness of Sinai, and camped in the wilderness; Israel camped there in front of the mountain. Then Moses went up to God; the Lord called to him from the mountain" (Exodus 19:1-3). Apparently, the Israelites camped in the desert facing the holy mountain. According to this description, the climb up to the mountaintop from the encampment must have been easily negotiated. This seems to correspond well with the layout at Har Karkom.

The Book of Numbers lists the names of stations of the Exodus and describes how the Israelites "encamped at Rephidim, where there was no water for the people to drink. And they departed from Rephidim, and pitched in the wilderness of Sinai" (Numbers 33:1-3). This undoubtedly refers to the encampment at the foot of the holy mountain, because Kivrot-Hataava, the following station along the route, was reached after the stay at Horeb (another name the Bible uses for Mt. Sinai; see Numbers 11:34).

A peculiar fact arises from this brief description: Having found no water at Rephidim, where there must have been a well, Moses turned toward a place in the desert that he probably knew had a good water source. Thus, the Biblical text suggests that even though the encampment at the foot of Mt. Sinai was in the desert and not in an oasis, there was still plenty of water there for the people to drink.

The situation described in Numbers 11 may apply to other places as well, but it is interesting to note that Har Karkom fits the description perfectly. There is an important waterhole on the plateau. In addition, in the western valley at the foot of the mountain, there are several waterholes (*gevim*) located below the cliffs. The rock there is quite impermeable and only a little rain is needed for the precipices above to become actual waterfalls. Around these waterholes are the remains of small artificial canals that must have been built to collect rainwater even more efficiently. When kept in good condition, these waterholes must have contained much more water than they are able to hold today.

The remains of campsites extend along Nahal Karkom (Wadi Ideid) for about 4.5 miles up to Beer Karkom (Bir Ideid), a perennial well where even during the summer the water level is only about 39 feet below ground level. Numerous important sites from the Bronze Age were found in this area. No doubt this desert region was able to provide sufficient drinking water for travelers throughout the entire year; even in this respect, Har Karkom satisfies one of the basic requirements for the location of Mt. Sinai.

Once we began looking for parallels between the Biblical descriptions of Mt. Sinai and our discoveries at Har Karkom, there seemed to be no end. For many years we had neglected the

This rock engraving depicts a grid divided into ten spaces. Although no writing or symbols appear on the rock, Anati speculates that the image may represent a rectangular stone tablet bearing the Ten Commandments.

Located along a rocky path, a large flint rock displays a twisting snake next to a staff. Author Anati wonders whether the graffito may be related to Exodus 7:8-12, in which Moses proves God's power to Pharaoh by turning a staff into a snake and back again.

Bible. Now we had to ask ourselves: What is the meaning of all these similarities? Are they just intriguing coincidences?

The principal obstacle to identifying Har Karkom with Mt. Sinai seemed to be the date.

If we accept the date scholars usually assign to the Exodus, then we must dismiss Har Karkom as a possible candidate for Mt. Sinai, because nothing has been found there indicating a human presence during the 13th century B.C. or anytime near this date. If Har Karkom was Mt. Sinai and if the Exodus did indeed occur at that time, we should have found at least some vestiges of the campsites of the Israelites and some evidence of cult activities on the mountain from that period. But our discoveries at Har Karkom belong to the third millennium B.C.

However, my own restudy of the archaeological materials, a reexamination prompted by our discoveries at Har Karkom, has led me to the conclusion that on this point the exegetes may be wrong.

Since I began surveying Har Karkom, I have studied the Bible very thoroughly. The Bible speaks of several peoples other than the Israelites who lived in the desert at the time of the Exodus and had contacts with the Israelites. The Amalekites, who populated the central Negev and the Kadesh-Barnea area, for example, tried to stop the Israelites from entering the Promised Land: "Then came Amalek, and fought with Israel in Rephidim" (Exodus 17:8). The Midianites were another people, related to the Hebrews through Moses, who had frequent contacts with the wandering tribes of Israel (see, for example, Exodus 18:5). If the Biblical accounts are indeed based on fact, some remains of desert peoples like the Amalekites and Midianites should have come to light during the numerous archaeological surveys and excavations carried out in this area, but precious little has been found. In all eastern Sinai and the southern Negev there are no traces whatever that might indicate a human presence during the 14th and 13th centuries B.C., except some Egyptian mines that are unrelated to the Exodus.

By contrast, the entire desert area traversed by the Israelites, as related in the Bible, has yielded abundant archaeological remains from what I call BAC, or the Bronze Age Complex—the period of the Early Bronze Age and Middle Bronze I, roughly the third millennium B.C.

Kadesh-Barnea must have been the main tribal center during the Exodus, yet it has no trace of a Late Bronze Age (and in particular of a 13th-century B.C.) occupation. On the other hand, significant and abundant remains from the BAC have been recovered there, materials that are quite similar to those we found at the foot of Har Karkom.

The first two cities conquered by Joshua—Jericho and Ai—did not exist in the Late Bronze Age. The archaeological excavations carried out there over several decades by various expeditions have shown that both have clear and dramatic evidence of destruction and burning during the period of the Bronze Age Complex. Such archaeological discoveries conform well to events described in the Bible.

Archaeological surveys carried on in Jordan by Nelson Glueck and others have shown, in the BAC period, colonization that fits the Biblical descriptions very well. Nothing of the sort is known in the Late Bronze Age.

We could continue with other examples. We could talk about the excellent parallels between descriptions in Exodus and in the Egyptian literature of the First Intermediate period, but we shall stop here. If the narration of Exodus has any relation to actual events, the archaeological evidence indicates that the Exodus could only have occurred in the period of the Bronze Age Complex, in the third millennium B.C. The traditional dating of the Exodus is simply wrong.

There is, however, another possibility: Some scholars question whether the Exodus ever occurred. For them, it is an aetiological story, created to provide Israel with a national history. I do not accept this. As the great Israeli archaeologist Yigael Yadin used to say, "What kind of people would invent for themselves a history of enslavement and escape from slavery?" We would expect the people to invent for themselves a more distinguished history.

But even if the Sinai event is an aetiological story, it must have drawn on elements of actual events. Some real events must have inspired the dramatic story of the holy mountain. It would be hard to find a better candidate for this mountain than Har Karkom.

Har Karkom was a holy mountain, a mountain of religious pilgrimage for a thousand years and more. This is strictly factual— and incontestable. The remains at the sites strikingly recall the story of Mt. Sinai in the Bible. But, is Har Karkom Mt. Sinai? The answer to this question is not factual, but conjectural. To say that it is Mt. Sinai requires a radical redating of the Exodus, and many scholars will be loathe to do this. But even if, to some scholars' minds, the date of the Exodus cannot be reconciled with the date of the archaeological remains on Har Karkom, the nagging question remains: Isn't there some connection between the two, between the unique event described so dramatically in the Bible and this unique holy mountain—unlike any other in the entire Sinai and Negev? Especially in light of the striking correspondences I have described, it seems to me that there must be a connection.

Much work undoubtedly remains to be done. But surely it is worthwhile raising questions.

1.   See Emmanuel Anati, *Palestine Before the Hebrews* (New York: Knopf, 1963), and *The Mountain of God* (New York: Rizzoli, 1986).

2.   A grant from the Fondazione C.A.B. of Brescia, Italy, supported our research from 1983 to 1984. Some private donors in the United States and in Europe have also contributed to our efforts. But, on the whole, fund-raising is one of the most depressing jobs for an archaeologist, and funds are never adequate. In Israel, the research was carried on within the framework of the Archaeological Survey of Israel, in collaboration with the Department of Antiquities and Museums of the Ministry of Education and Culture.

The participants in the research reported in this essay, published first in 1985, included Emmanuel Anati, director; Ariela Fradkin Anati, secretary; Gigi Cottinelli, Tiziana Cittadini, Ivonne Riano and Gianbattista Cottinelli, architects; Olga Pirelli, conservator; Avraham Hay and Daniel Anati, photographers; Larryn Diamond, geologist; Paola Pirelli and Giovanna Davini, botanists; Nancy Wise, recorder; Lucia Bellaspiga, Ida Mailland and Laura Valmadre, assistants. In addition, several of the expeditions were assisted by volunteers from the Field School of Mizpe Ramon; Gideon Avni and other archaeologists and guides from the Israel Department of Antiquities also helped us. In Italy, the cartography was carried on by Stefano Farina and Alessandra Angeloni; the analysis of aerial photographs by Tamar Piperna, the computerization of data by Franca Angeli and Antonio Guereira. A special acknowledgement is due to Rudolph Cohen, then regional archaeologist of the Southern Region, and to Avi Eitan, then director of the Department of Antiquities, for their support.

3.   See Rudolph Cohen, "The Mysterious MB I People: Does the Exodus Tradition in the Bible Preserve Their Entry into Canaan?" *Biblical Archaeology Review*, July/August 1983.

Har Karkom Update

Emmanuel Anati

Much has happened at Har Karkom since 1985, when I first published the accompanying chapter as an article in *Biblical Archaeology Review*. Our exploration of the site has continued steadily in the years since, and the mountain is still yielding remarkable finds.[1]

One of the most significant discoveries, made in 1992, is a Paleolithic "sanctuary" dating, based on the age of the flint implements found there, to the Upper Paleolithic Period, some 35,000 to 40,000 years ago. The sanctuary makes clear that Har Karkom was not just a Bronze Age cult site, as was previously assumed, but had been a holy site ever since the arrival of the first *Homo sapiens*. This means Har Karkom is one of the oldest high-places where human beings are known to have worshiped. Har Karkom, it is now clear, has always been a sacred mountain.

In 1993 new features of Har Karkom's plateau came to light as aerial surveys identified large geoglyphs, or surface drawings made either with pebbles or with the clearing of stones. Some of the geoglyphs are simply lines; others represent geometric arrangements or abstract shapes; still others depict quadrupeds, measuring up to 100 feet long. For years the expedition members had walked across these figures without realizing they were there, because the images are hardly readable from the surface. Their function is still a mystery. Perhaps they were offerings to a celestial entity or representations of holy domains symbolized by the images.

In 1994 a cave in the sloping edges of Har Karkom yielded evidence of habitation by a single individual. The dweller had arranged a row of stones around a flattened area of sand, presumably for sleeping, of 2 by 5.5 feet—just the size of a single bed. The cave held remains of a fireplace, sherds of a water jar from the transition phase between the Early and Middle Bronze Ages (c. 2200 B.C.), two flint blades and a bone spatula. Bones found near ashes indicate that the cave dweller ate the meat and eggs of birds such as quail and partridge, as well as small mammals. From the remains of his diet we know that he lived there during a period when these birds were migrating—either autumn or spring. We also found ostrich eggshells, which provided a carbon-14 dating of about 2125 B.C. (4130 +/-50 Before Present). We will never know the name of this "hermit," but his cave provides an archaeological parallel to the Biblical episode in which Moses "went up to the mountain; there he stayed forty days and forty nights" (Exodus 24:18).

Thanks to the cave at Har Karkom, we now know that hermits did indeed live alone in the desert in the Bronze Age.

Over the years, more and more rock engravings have come to light, from pre-Neolithic early hunter art to Bedouin graffiti, including several Bronze Age images of scenes that we believe have parallels in the Pentateuch (details appear on our Web site, www.harkarkom.com).

In 1998 we excavated a peculiar tumulus, or heap of stones, measuring 23 feet in diameter and almost 10 feet high. Once the heap of stones had been removed, it was found that it did not contain a burial as we had thought, but an altar, on top of which was positioned a white stone cut into the shape of a half-circle or half-moon. It appears to be a *gal-ed*, or heap of testimony, dedicated to the moon, or more likely, to the moon-god Sin. Flint implements with typical fan scrapers date the tumulus to the Early Bronze Age. The moonstone is 26 inches long and weights almost 100 pounds. Traces of ash around the altar indicate that a fire was lit here.

The tumulus was located on the edge of the eastern ridge of the mountain. Just 650 feet below it, on a natural terrace, were the stone basements of a three-room courtyard. Here we discovered the same kind of flint implements associated with the altar, indicating that this was the dwelling of the people who once used the altar.

In more recent years, other such dedicatory tumuli have been identified, including one along the main trail leading from the eastern valley to the plateau. It is located at the very spot where the summit of Har Karkom first comes into view for walkers on the trail. Beneath this tumulus was a heavy, altar-like, rectangular stone balanced on a few smaller stones. A stone circle of about 23 feet in diameter was built around it. Again, the presence of ashes indicates the use of fire. On top was a black stone engraved with six disks. We do not know what this stone-covered monument commemorated.

Several ancient trails leading up the mountain from the desert were identified during the survey. In 1999, we found a trail on the eastern side that included several ceremonial stations, dating to the Early Bronze Age. Two of the stations had a standing pillar in front of a clearing; one had a large stone circle surrounding fallen boulders; several others had clearings and rock engravings. Apparently during the Early Bronze Age, people going up to or coming down from the plateau stopped along the way to perform various rituals.

In 1980, when we started our survey of Har Karkom, the ten rock-art sites that I had discovered in 1955 were the only archaeological finds known in the area. The past 24 years of archaeological expeditions have revealed ancient villages and campsites, worship sites, rock-art centers, rock shelters, burial grounds, geoglyphs and more. We have now recorded more than 1,200 archaeological sites.

In 1983, we suggested that Har Karkom might be connected to Biblical Mt. Sinai. The proposal inspired vigorous debate among Biblical experts, historians and Near Eastern archaeologists. (This debate is summarized on our

Web site, www.harkarkom.com, and in various issues of the *Bulletin of the Center for Prehistoric Studies*.) The controversy is still not resolved. There is no question, however, that this mountain, with its plateau of shrines and its valleys dotted with ancient villages, was a desert gathering place for multitudes despite the meager natural and economic resources of the surrounding area. Further, to the best of our knowledge, Har Karkom is the only mountain in the Sinai peninsula or the Negev where there is so much archaeological evidence of sacred worship from the Paleolithic Period to the Bronze Age.

The tumulus dedicated to the god Sin may hint at a possible signification of the name Sinai. But this is speculation. The numerous rock engravings showing mythic themes that seem to parallel Biblical episodes are suggestive analogies, but not proofs. The importance of the site as a Bronze Age holy mountain is similarly intriguing, but not conclusive.

Analysis of the Biblical description of the topography and location of Mt. Sinai may prove to be more conclusive. In my opinion, the Exodus itinerary described in the Bible must have made sense topographically when it was compiled, in the first millenium B.C., by people who knew the area.

From 1952 to 1954, I conducted the first archaeological survey of the Central Negev highlands. In 1989, and again in 1992, I traced the various Exodus routes that have been proposed, departing from the Land of Goshen, in the Nile Delta, and traveling through the Egyptian Sinai, the Israeli Negev, and Jordan. I now believe that the list of way stations in the biblical narrative makes good geographical and topographical sense. Indeed, I believe I have identified the location of several sites mentioned in Exodus, including Marah, Elim and Rephidim, where the Israelites stopped on their way to Mt. Sinai.[2]

Further, the Israelites' itinerary after Mt. Sinai meshes well with what we know about the area around Har Karkom. A close reading of the Biblical text indicates that Mt. Sinai stands south of Maale Akrabim, between the Arava Valley and the central Negev highlands. Har Karkom fits these coordinates perfectly.

We now know that Har Karkom was a holy mountain for millennia. The archaeological remains and the geographical evidence from the site seem to give new life to the Biblical accounts. No other mountain in the Negev and Sinai area corresponds so well to Biblical Mt. Sinai. Our continuing research makes me increasingly confident that the Bible's compilers were referring to this mountain when they wrote about Mt. Sinai.

1. The main discoveries have been described in Emmanuel Anati, *The Mountain of God* (New York: Rizzoli, 1986) and *The Riddle of Mount Sinai* (Capo di Ponte, Italy: Edizioni del Centro, 2001), and most recently, on our Web site: www.harkarkom.com.

2. Anati, *Esodo, tra mito e storia* [*Exodus: Between Myth and History*] (Capo di Ponte, Italy: Edizioni del Centro, 1997).

CHAPTER 5

False Conclusions
Identification of Har Karkom Flawed

Israel Finkelstein

In the previous chapter, Italian archaeologist Emmanuel Anati argues that he has found Mt. Sinai, the "Mountain of God," on a ridge in the western edge of the Negev Highlands, 4 miles from the Egyptian border.

Anati's search for Mt. Sinai (as presented here and in his oversized, colorful and expensive book *The Mountain of God)* is an anachronistic vestige from the 19th century.[1] The only difference is that Anati's work is illustrated with beautiful color pictures. The academic community—archaeologists and Biblical scholars alike—will ignore his revelation. The problem, however, is that many lay people with a genuine interest in the Bible and Biblical archaeology will be vulnerable to this kind of material, especially because the author is relatively well known, his subject matter is magnetic and his presentation is beautiful.

To review his work is, in a way, a disgraceful task. But it is important to do—both to save the trampled honor of archaeology as a serious scientific discipline and to protect the innocent mind of the lay public from these kinds of theories.

The search for Mt. Sinai, the Mountain of God, was a popular quest in the 19th century, when travelers and explorers roamed the Sinai Peninsula looking for footsteps of the Children of Israel. However, decades of research, even by great scholars like Edward Palmer and Edward Robinson, made little, if any, progress. Finally, in about the 1920s, the question was laid to rest. The simple reason was that not a shred of evidence was found that cast any light on the Biblical Exodus narratives.

The present state of research on the Exodus can be summarized as follows:

The only source that provides any direct evidence concerning the Exodus and the desert wanderings of the Children of Israel is the Bible. There is not a single direct reference for these Biblically described events in the rich Egyptian material, although an abundance of documents from the 19th Egyptian dynasty do reflect the general conditions that prevailed in the eastern Nile Delta at the time most scholars would date the reality behind the Exodus narratives. Nor is there any real archaeological evidence concerning the Biblical narrative in Sinai or the Negev.

The Bible refers to numerous place-names—toponyms is the scholars' word—on the route of the Exodus. Of all these toponyms mentioned in connection with the Israelites' desert wanderings only two can be securely identified—Kadesh-Barnea (Ein el-Qudeirat in the eastern part of north Sinai) and Ezion-Geber (Tell el-Kheleifeh near Eilat). A few other places—Pi-hahiroth, Baal-zephon and Migdol (see Exodus 14 and Numbers 33)—may be located in the northeastern corner of the ancient Nile Delta (present-day northwestern Sinai). However, of the numerous other toponyms, not one can be located.

Three factors determine the identification of Biblical (or any other ancient) sites: (1) the geographical context of the

Biblical reference, (2) the archaeological finds at the proposed site (that is, whether the proposed site was occupied in the particular period when it appears in the text), and (3) the possible preservation, in some form, of the ancient toponym in a later, even modern, name. None of these factors is present in the dozens of desert-stations on the Exodus route. From the Bible itself, there is absolutely no way to determine in what part of the southern deserts extending from the Negev to the southern tip of Sinai these sites are located. Nor do any archaeological finds in Sinai help to identify any of these sites. (Admittedly, one can claim that the Israelites were nomads and hence did not leave behind any remains.) Finally, we cannot rely on later or modern desert place-names to provide any help (as we do in settled areas) because there was no continuity of occupation in the desert. Thus, the proposed identification of Biblical Hazeroth, for example, with Ein Huderah, southwest of Eilat, is a mere desert mirage; the modern names of dozens of sites in Sinai resemble this ancient toponym—Ein el-Ahdar, Wadi Ahdar, etc.

Moreover, we must not forget that the Biblical material was assembled centuries after the supposed events took place. Without denigrating the importance of the Exodus narratives for the faith of ancient Israel, we simply cannot treat these Biblical narratives as straightforward history. We must understand the historical and religious background against which these traditions crystallized at a later date, during the period of the Israelite monarchy, hundreds of years after the supposed events that the narratives describe could have taken place.

For all these reasons, the day when explorers rushed to the desert with the Bible in one hand and a spade in the other is long gone. In fact, the only "historical" tradition about Mt. Sinai dates from the Byzantine period, in the fourth to seventh centuries A.D., at a time when a host of holy places in southern Sinai and elsewhere were "identified." At that time the location of Mt. Sinai crystallized near the Monastery of St. Catherine, located at the foot of what is now called Jebel Musa. But this identification must be evaluated against the background of the events in the eastern provinces of the Roman world in the second to fourth centuries, as well as against the environmental aspects of the region.

Taking all these factors into consideration, it is not surprising that we now know no more about the Exodus and the desert wanderings of the Israelites than we did 150 years ago.

Until new archaeological materials are found, however—an extremely unlikely possibility—no serious archaeological research on the Exodus and the desert wanderings can be carried out. It is therefore regrettable that once again we are witness to a romantic expedition exploring the southern wilderness, choosing a peak that has not previously been a candidate, and then trying to convince lay people that Mt. Sinai has been found. Unfortunately, some gullible members of the lay public are always ready to accept simple *deus ex machina* solutions, rather than undertaking the painful struggle required to deal with a complex problem that has no clear-cut answer.

Anati's candidate for the Mountain of God is Har Karkom, a flat ridge surrounded by cliffs on the southwestern edge of the Negev Highlands. His evidence is that on the ridge and around it are a large number of small sites dating to the third millennium B.C., as well as an impressive concentration of rock drawings. Anati interprets some of these sites as a temple and a sacred group of twelve stones, etc. He understands some of the rock drawings as depicting cultic scenes. He then attempts to fit the Biblical descriptions into this setting.

It is not difficult to do. The Biblical material can be used almost anywhere in the south: in the Negev, near St. Catherine's monastery in Sinai, in northern Sinai, in northwestern Sinai near the Gulf of Suez, etc.

Let us look at Anati's archaeological "evidence" that supposedly supports his conclusion. I do not intend to comment on his treatment of the Biblical material; Anati is, after all, an archaeologist, not a Biblical scholar. But there is another reason why it is unnecessary to comment on the way Anati handles the Biblical materials: Once we expose the false archaeological evidence, his whole theory collapses.

At the outset, Anati must confront a "minor" chronological problem: The emergence of Israel in Canaan occurred in the 13th to 12th century B.C. But Anati dates his sites around Har Karkom almost 1,500 years earlier than that. The date for the emergence of Israel in Canaan has been fixed by data accumulated from a host of excavations and surveys conducted throughout the country since the 1920s, and is now so well established that it cannot be successfully challenged. This date is also supported by the earliest extra-Biblical reference to Israel—in the famous Merneptah stele, a hieroglyphic inscription that dates to the year 1207 B.C.

Because Anati dates his sites near Har Karkom to the third millennium B.C., he must conclude that the Sinai narratives in the Bible reflect a third millennium tradition. But he nowhere explains how this third millennium tradition survived until the first millennium B.C. in the memory of people in Jerusalem (where the material was compiled), without any continuity of activity at Har Karkom!

A word of caution should also be noted about the large number of sites Anati has supposedly found at Har Karkom. In arid zones, sites tend to spread over vast areas. How many sites there actually are depends on how you count them. I suspect that at Har Karkom there are no more than a few dozen real sites, plus a large number of rock drawings.

Moreover, the concentration of these sites near Har Karkom is by no means unique. Similar clusters of sites can be found in other parts of the Negev. Indeed, the density of sites per square mile is much higher in other areas of the Negev Highlands than at Har Karkom.

Anati fails to mention the fact that sites from the Early Bronze Age II (c. 2850-2650 B.C.) have been found throughout the southern deserts—from Arad in the north to southern Sinai in the south. Nor does he mention that sites from the Intermediate Bronze Age (c. 2350-2200 B.C.; some archaeologists refer to this period as Early Bronze IV or Middle Bronze I) are found all over the Negev Highlands. The sites near Har Karkom are therefore part of a broader archaeological-historical phenomenon. Anati refers to none of the important works published by Itzhaq Beit-Arieh, Rudolph Cohen and William Dever that describe this phenomenon and the results of intensive research conducted in Sinai and the Negev in recent years. Nor does Anati refer to the extensive surveys and rescue excavations conducted in the Negev by the Israel Department of Antiquities (now the Israel Antiquities Authority) and the Archaeological Survey of Israel since 1979. In short, Anati deals with the sites at Har Karkom as if they were the only sites in the whole area with evidence of human activity; he ignores the entire archaeological context of the Har Karkom phenomenon.

Next: In my view, it is extremely tricky, probably impossible, to date rock drawings accurately. Most of the scenes depict daily life of the desert people, herding flocks, say, or hunting. It is difficult, if not impossible, to compare such scenes to securely dated material. Dating by the patina is also baseless. The patina does not provide a reliable dating mechanism because the production of the patina depends on factors other than age, such as microclimate. The most reasonable assumption is that these rock drawings were carved by local pastoral nomads over a long time, rather than in one archaeological period.

Anati tells us that Har Karkom was occupied in some periods, separated by periods of "hiatus" when there was no occupation. This reflects an outmoded, naive view of the history of the occupation of the southern deserts. Sinai and the Negev are not like certain areas in Saudi Arabia or the Sahara, where the harsh environment either prevents human occupation or makes it extremely difficult. Ecological niches in the Negev Highlands and the high mountains of southern Sinai, as well as other parts of the region, readily permit human activity, based on pastoral nomadism, hunting and seasonal agriculture. Accordingly people lived here continuously, but unlike areas of settled occupation, they rarely left any archaeological remains. The exceptions are the few periods when the desert inhabitants built stone structures. The question of why they did so at certain times and not others is beyond the scope of this article. But the point here is that there were no periods without human occupation and that the rock art at Har Karkom may well represent human activity from periods without other archaeological remains.

The chronological term that Anati uses, BAC (Bronze Age Complex), to cover both Early Bronze Age and Intermediate Bronze Age sites is misleading: Early Bronze sites and Intermediate Bronze sites can be distinguished from one another in scientific excavations and often even in surveys, when conducted by trained archaeologists.

Anati's interpretations of some of the finds (and in a few cases, these are not archaeological finds at all, but "innocent" natural phenomena) belong to the world of faith, rather than the world of archaeology: According to Anati, broken stone slabs represent the tradition of the stone tablets Moses received on Mt. Sinai. Sites around the Har Karkom ridge are interpreted as the encampments of the Israelites. Rock drawings depict "the serpent" and "the staff" in the tradition of the Bible. Other rock drawings, he says, depict standing stones or other "Biblical" scenes. The truth is that all this is in the eye of the beholder.

Anati also mistreats toponyms. Two examples will suffice. In his book, he identifies Biblical Hormah with Nessana, a Nabatean-Byzantine site with absolutely no earlier material. He uses names like Paran and Zin for areas near Har Karkom without any discussion of the problem of their location.

To sum up, Anati's research reflects not a trace of the elementary skills required by the scientific discipline of archaeology. Anati fails to distinguish between (1) finds, (2) the interpretation of these finds and (3) a synthesis of the finds with the historical source (in this case the Bible).

Now let us turn from Anati's heavenly theories to an earthly discussion; that is, to a rational explanation of the Har Karkom finds.

After eliminating the far-fetched interpretations and the misleading information, we are left with some real facts: Here is a ridge in the Negev with more human occupation sites than found on the immediately neighboring ridges. In addition,

Har Karkom differs from the main parts of the Negev Highlands by having a much larger number of rock drawings than at other sites.

How can we explain this overall phenomenon?

The answer lies in the patterns of pastoral existence found in the Negev Highlands, as well as in certain parts of central and southern Sinai—a kind of pastoral existence still reflected in subsistence patterns of 20th-century Bedouin. The ecology of these environments requires short-distance, seasonal migrations. There is, in effect, a seasonal vertical movement, from the lower regions in winter to the higher ecological niches in summer. Higher elevations get more precipitation and hence provide more pasturage for flocks. In the winter the pastoral sheep- or goat-herding nomads would exploit the pastures in the lower areas, which sprout earlier because of their warmer temperatures. In the spring these pastoral nomads would move to the higher regions. In the western part of the Negev Highlands, the winter-pasture areas were to the west, in the plains of northwestern Sinai. In the summer the flocks were taken eastwards, to the ridges of Har Horesha, Har Harif, Har Loz, Har Ha-me'ara, Har Saggi—and Har Karkom. This is the reason for the large concentration of sites along this line. Har Karkom had a special advantage: A nearby well (Be'er Karkom) supplied water for the flocks. (This, by the way, explains why most of the sites Anati found are scattered west of Har Karkom.) The water source of Ein Ha-me'ara played a similar role further north. The explanation for the relatively large number of rock drawings at Har Karkom should also be sought in this pastoral or nomadic way of life: The steep cliffs that surrounded the ridge probably made the site more attractive to herders because they could control the flocks more easily. As they whiled away their time at this popular site, they made their drawings on the rock faces.

To return for a moment to the Biblical Mountain of God: The importance of the Exodus narrative lies in its moral code and in the role it played in Israel's development and in the tradition of Western civilization. The Biblical account was never meant to be a guide to enthusiastic archaeological expeditions. Let us leave the Mountain of God to rest in peace. For those who cannot resist temptation, let Indiana Jones deliver the goods.

---

1.   Emmanuel Anati, *The Mountain of God* (New York: Rizzoli, 1986).

"In the sixth year of Hezekiah, which was the ninth year of King Hoshea of Israel, Samaria was taken. The king of Assyria carried the Israelites away to Assyria, settled them in Halah, on the Habor, the river of Gozan and in the cities of the Medes, because they did not obey the voice of the Lord their God but transgressed his covenant—all that Moses the servant of the Lord had commanded; they neither listened nor obeyed."

(2 Kings 18:10-12)

Part IV

THE TEN LOST TRIBES

The twelve sons of the patriarch Jacob (who is also called Israel) were the eponymous ancestors of the twelve tribes of Israel. After the Conquest, each tribe settled in a different region. For roughly two centuries, from the late eleventh to the late tenth century B.C., the tribes were united under kings Saul, David and Solomon. But after the death of King Solomon in about 920 B.C., the United Kingdom of Israel fell apart, and the twelve tribes were divided into two nations: the southern kingdom of Judah, which had its capital in Jerusalem and which consisted of the tribes of Judah and Benjamin; and the northern kingdom of Israel, which had its capital at Samaria and which included the tribes of Reuben, Simeon, Levi, Issachar, Zebulun, Dan, Naphtali, Gad, Asher, Joseph (and the tribes of his sons Manasseh and Ephraim) and Benjamin.

In 721 B.C., the northern kingdom of Israel was conquered and destroyed by the Assyrians, and the Israelites were deported. The same fate befell the kingdom of Judah at the hands of the Babylonians in 587 B.C., when Jerusalem was destroyed and the Babylonian captivity began. The Babylonian captives were allowed to return fifty years later, however, as decreed by the Persian emperor Cyrus (see 2 Chronicles 36:22-23). But what of the ten tribes that had been deported following the Assyrian conquest of the northern kingdom of Israel? They were never heard from again. Or were they? In the following chapter, Howard W. Goodkind assesses modern theories about ancient Israelites coming to the Americas. Chapter 7 summarizes recent archaeological evidence that some northern tribesmen may have simply settled in Judah. Finally, Chapter 8 assesses the merits of Hillel Halkin's much-publicized book claiming that a remnant of the tribe of Manasseh survives today on the Indo-Burmese border.

CHAPTER 6

How Lord Kingsborough Lost His Fortune

Looking for the Lost Tribes Among the Maya

Howard W. Goodkind

In 1837, Edward King, Viscount of Kingsborough, sat languishing in a Dublin debtor's prison, sick and impoverished. His fortune was gone, and he was suffering from typhus. Within a month, he would die in prison, at the age of 42. He had, some would say, squandered his patrimony in publishing a series of books on the peoples of Mesoamerica, the region of central and southern Mexico, Guatemala, Belize and northern Honduras where native civilizations thrived before the Spanish Conquest.

Kingsborough had spent 18 years producing his nine-volume *The Antiquities of Mexico: Comprising Facsimiles of Ancient Mexican Paintings and Hieroglyphics...Together with the Monuments of New Spain* (1830). The results were, quite simply, stupendous. Each massive volume is roughly 2 feet square, weighs about 65 pounds, and consists of hundreds of pages of text and magnificent illustrations in color and black-and-white, painstakingly copied by a talented artist named Augustine Aglio. The cost of £40,000 to produce the set was a truly enormous sum in terms of the currency of the time, when a family could live quite well on £500 a year.

Kingsborough's impact on Mesoamerican archaeology was immense. Seminal Indian documents, such as the Dresden Codex and the Mendoza Codex, first appeared in facsimile form in Kingsborough's set. He had searched around the world for Indian codices (long strips of bark, deerskin or agave paper, covered with gesso and folded like screens) and 16th-century Spanish accounts of Mesoamerican history and culture, which were also illustrated in his volumes. Kingsborough's work remained a prime source for researchers for well over a hundred years, when fine photographic reproductions of the same documents became available.

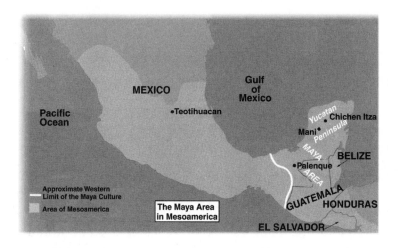

According to one story, Kingsborough's interest in Mesoamerican culture was sparked by seeing a rare Aztec codex in the Bodleian Library while a student at Oxford. This interest, which soon became a consuming passion to the exclusion of almost everything else, involved much more than pure scholarship. Kingsborough was convinced that the Mesoamerican Indians were direct descendants of the ten tribes of Israel, who were exiled by the Assyrians in 721 B.C. and then lost to history.

The idea that the Indians of Mesoamerica were the ten lost tribes did not originate with Lord Kingsborough. For hundreds of years scholars had speculated about the whereabouts of the tribes of Israel, hypothesizing China, Japan, and even the British Isles. When the Spanish clergy arrived in the New World with the

Conquistadores, they heard Indian accounts of ancient ancestors who came from the east. Their legends sounded remarkably like the Biblical account of creation and the story of the Tower of Babel, and the Spaniards immediately jumped to the conclusion that these early settlers were the ten lost tribes.

The notion spread quickly during the 16th century. Among European scholars who became its ardent supporters were the Spanish clergymen Juan de Torquemada (not to be confused with his relative, Tomás de Torquemada, terror of the Inquisition); Bishop Diego de Landa, who lived among the Maya; DeLery, a French writer, who put forth the idea in 1556; and Father Durán,

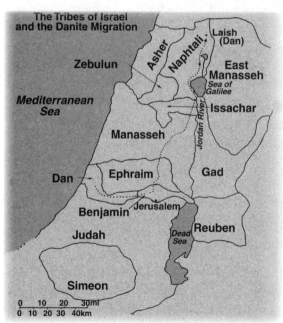

who speculated in 1585 about the similarities between Indian rites and those of the ancient Jews.[1]

Two hypotheses were debated among Spanish scholars as to how the Israelites came to the New World. Toward the end of the 16th century, Gregorio García in his *Origen de los indios de el nuevo mondo* made the case for a Hebrew migration by sea. José de Acosta, a remarkably perceptive Jesuit priest, argued that the migration of men to the New World was land-based. Acosta was struck by the resemblance of New World Indians to Orientals, especially the Tartars. In his *Historia natural y moral de las indias*, Acosta postulated the existence of a land "bridge" long before anyone knew of the Bering Strait. This migration theory is accepted today by 99.99 percent of archaeologists and anthropologists. Of course, the accepted modern theory does not include the idea that the immigrants who crossed to the New World were Israelites.[2]

In 1650, an Englishman, Thomas Thorowgood, offered a series of arguments to "prove" that the Indians were the long-lost tribes. In his book *Jewes in America or probabilities that the Americans are of that race*, he wrote:

> "Muteczuma the great King of Mexico in an oration made to his nobles and people ... reminds his country-men that they heard from their forefathers, how they were strangers in that land, and by a great prince very long ago brought thither in a fleet."

According to Thorowgood, the Mexican emperor also said that God made one man and one woman, rained bread from heaven during a famine, and gave water from a rock during a drought. He then asked his readers to explain how the Aztecs could possibly recount the history of Israel if they were not Jews.

Thorowgood also offered these additional "proofs":[3]

- New England Indians separated their women in a wig-wam during "feminine seasons."

- Aztecs, like Jews, washed themselves often.

- Indians washed strangers' feet, as the ancient Jews did.

- Indians washed their newborn infants and nursed their own children, both Jewish traits.

- Indians were "given much to weeping, their women especially, and at burials, this being in fashion among the Jewes."

Lord Kingsborough's arguments were similar to Thorowgood's. They are contained in an enormous body of notes appended to the various Mesoamerican documents illustrated in his set of volumes. All are intended to convince the reader that the Indians were the lost tribes of Israel.

On occasion Kingsborough's arguments are somewhat more sophisticated than Thorowgood's; at other times, he sim-ply abandons all pretense to scientific objectivity and expresses his undisguised anti-Semitism. For example, he tells us that "Of all the nations who ever inhabited the globe … the Jews were by far the most hard-hearted and barbarous." He quotes Sir William Penn, who says of the Indians: "When you look upon them, you would think yourself in the Jews' quarter in London. Their eyes are little and black, like the Jews." And he frequently quotes Torquemada the theologian, who compared the severity of the way the Aztecs treated their unruly children with the Mosaic laws that supposedly give parents the power of life and death over their children.

Some of Kingsborough's arguments are offered in a more objective vein:

- The Aztecs placed great store in dreams and visions. This trait, according to Kingsborough, is clearly Oriental and common to the peoples in the area around Palestine.

- The general Aztec fast is called Atamal, which means water and bread. For Kingsborough, this is reminiscent of the unleavened bread Jews eat on Passover.

- The Aztecs blew a "trumpet" on festivals as Jews do. (The Aztecs made their trumpet from a conch shell; the ancient Hebrews usually used a ram's horn.)

- Kingsborough noted an Aztec migration legend concerning how their ancestors left their island home named Aztlan (which he compared with the Jews leaving Egypt). The Aztecs were led by the brothers Huitziton and Tecpatzin (like Moses and Aaron), who were attended by their sister, Quitaztli or Malinalli. The name Malinalli reminded Kingsborough of Miriam, Moses' sister.

The list could go on and on. Kingsborough was tireless and compiled an enormous number of detailed, imaginative arguments to bolster his case. Kingsborough also argued that Jesus reappeared in the New World as Quetzalcoatl, the Indian feathered serpent god, a contention we shall meet up with again later in this article.

Despite the porous nature of these arguments, the belief that Mesoamerican Indians are the descendants of the lost tribes has been enormously influential—and beneficial—in modern

Codices–The Historical and Religious Records of the Ancient Mesoamericans

Some Mesoamerican civilizations recorded their history and beliefs in pictorial images and hieroglyphic writing on strips of pounded fig bark or on deerskin. Before being painted with natural pigments, the long strips of bark or deerskin were laid out and coated with a fine white stucco. Color was applied, and then the sections were folded, fan-fashion.

Only four Mayan codices survived the Spanish conquest. Three of them are now in libraries in Dresden, Madrid and Paris. The fourth codex, written by the Toltec-Maya Indians, is now called the Grolier Codex because it was first exhibited in 1971 at the Grolier Club in New York. This codex belonged to a private collector in Mexico and apparently was found in a wooden box in a cave near Tortuguero, Chiapas, sometime within the previous 20 years.

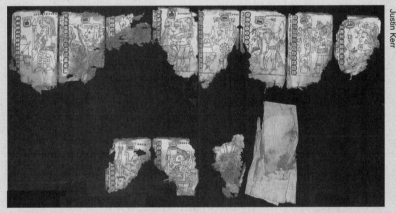

Justin Kerr

The Grolier Codex (the array of pages are shown here) describes the various cycles of the planet Venus and rituals associated with these cycles.

The paucity of surviving Mayan codices may be attributed in part to the religious zeal of the 16th-century bishop of Yucatan, Fray Diego de Landa, who tried to obliterate all traces of Maya religion. On July 12, 1562, de Landa directed the destruction of a priceless collection of Maya codices discovered in the Yucatan town of Mani. He ordered the burning of these books because, as he later wrote, they "contain[ed] nothing in which was not to be seen superstitions and lies of the devil." However, to his credit, de Landa wrote numerous descriptions of Mayan sites; his book *Relación de las cosas de Yucatan* remains an excellent source of information about the life and beliefs of the Maya.

Mesoamerican archaeology. Some of the finest archaeological work in southeastern Mexico has been conducted by a Mormon organization, the New World Archaeological Foundation (NWAF). Although the Mormons do not claim that the Mesoamerican Indians are descended from the ten lost tribes, they do believe that the Israelites came to America and founded the pre-Columbian civilizations, as is written in the *Book of Mormon.*

In 1842, Joseph Smith, founder of the Mormon church, read *Incidents of Travel in Central America, Chiapas, and Yucatan* by John Lloyd Stephens. On the basis of Stephens's book, Smith became convinced that the ancient cities described in the *Book of Mormon* were in Guatemala (which included, at that time, parts of Mexico).

According to Mormon belief, three different groups migrated to the New World. The earliest was the Jaredites, who came from Iraq to Mexico at the time of the Tower of Babel in about 2800 B.C. The second was the Nephites, who arrived in the sixth century B.C. and lived in Middle America. The third was the Lamanites, who came at about the same time as the Nephites, and who were dark-skinned relations of the Nephites. There is no mention of the Jaredites, Nephites and Lamanites prior to the *Book of Mormon. The Book of Mormon* describes a war between the Nephites and the Lamanites in the fourth century A.D., during which the Nephites were totally destroyed in a struggle that lasted 65 years. The Lamanites became the American Indians.[4] Over the years, many Mormon archaeologists have accepted the *Book of Mormon* as an accurate, historical account of the New World peoples between about 2000 B.C. and 421 A.D. Although the *Book of Mormon* itself gives no specific dates, the chronology has been developed by Mormon scholars, who place the early migrations in what they call the Formative Period (1500 B.C.-150 A.D.). That is why the NWAF has concentrated its efforts on the Formative Period.

As one of the most distinguished Mesoamerican archaeologists, Michael Coe, has observed, it would be difficult to find a trained archaeologist who is not a Mormon who believes that the Mesoamerican Indians are descendants of the Israelites who came to the New World in the three migrations detailed in the *Book of Mormon.* Indeed, according to Coe, quite a few Mormon archaeologists have also abandoned these beliefs.

Much of what we read in the *Book of Mormon* is not very persuasive. Coe cites many instances: For example, we are told that the horse was brought to the New World by the Jaredites and/or the Nephites. But the horse was extinct in the New World from about 7000 B.C. until it was brought back by the Spaniards. The Jaredites and/or the Nephites are also credited with bringing metallurgy to the New World. But the working of metal based on smelting and casting appears in Mesoamerica no earlier than 800 A.D. According to Mormon belief, the famous Mayan center of Palenque was a Nephite city. However, again as Coe points out, we now know that Palenque was built later than 600 A.D., 215 years after the Nephites had disappeared, according to the Mormons' own chronology. In general, there is little similarity between the *Book of Mormon*'s description of the New World between 2000 B.C. and 421 A.D. and what we know about the culture of the ancient Indians.[5]

In some respects, Joseph Smith reflects the 19th-century milieu in which he wrote. Smith, like others of his time, believed that ancient Indian burial and temple mounds in the midwestern and southeastern United States had been built by a fair-skinned race rather than by the dark-skinned natives found by Columbus. As Coe has noted, there is more than a hint of 19th-century racism in this unwillingness to believe that dark-skinned peoples were capable of such sophistication.

Looking at the Indian cultures as a whole, it is indeed difficult to accept any connection between them and the lost tribes of Israel—although admittedly it is easier to speak with assurance in the light of scholarly advances, especially during the last 50 years, that enable us to date much more securely the history and development of their cultures. These advances in chronology are due largely to breakthroughs in our knowledge of Mesoamerican writing systems and to the fine-tuning of carbon-14 dating.

Until the early part of this century, it was thought that the oldest North American culture was represented by the Maya. Now, as a result of excellent carbon-14 dates and our ability to read the inscriptions on stone stelae found in southern Mexico and Guatemala, we know that the Olmec preceded the Maya by more than a thousand years.

We can trace the development of the hunter-gatherers, through the stages of agriculture and urbanized living, to a time about 2,000 years ago when Mesoamericans became compulsive record-keepers.

At least two different systems of recording time were developed, both intermeshing in a complex relationship that now makes it possible to determine, at least during the first nine centuries of the Common Era, the precise day when an event took place.

The calendar known as the Long Count was probably invented by the Olmec in the first century B.C. For reasons we do not understand, the count of days begins with August 13, 3114 B.C., and continues, day by day, until the Maya stopped keeping records in about 900 A.D. When we find a stela or wall mural bearing a Long Count inscription, we know the exact date referred to by the scribe.

The second calendric system, called the Calendar Round, was based on a 52-year cycle; it, too, goes back to very early times but was still being used by the Aztecs when the Spanish Conquistadores arrived in the 16th century. The Calendar Round consists of two meshing calendars, so arranged that each named day—for example, 1 Kan 1 Pop—is repeated only once every 52 years. The Aztecs were terrified that the world would be destroyed at the end of each 52-year cycle.[6]

As a result of our refined knowledge of these ancient calendars, we can now determine with considerable certainty when each successive culture made its appearance on the Mesoamerican stage. We can also trace the development of religious beliefs as they passed from one culture to another.

With this knowledge, it should be relatively simple to spot the arrival of the Israelites. Yet there is no sign of them anywhere.

Moreover, the pantheon of gods in all of these Mesoamerican cultures is bewilderingly crowded—especially in the case of the Aztecs and Maya. This would certainly be a strange heritage from an ancient people renowned for having introduced monotheism to the civilized world.

Many of the Mesoamerican gods are bizarre by Old Testament standards. For example, the god K of the Maya, later known as Tezcatlipoca in the Aztec religion, is pictured with a missing foot and a serpent emerging from the stump of his leg. The foot is missing because one of the stars in the constellation Ursa Major that represents the god disappears for a time below the horizon in the latitude of Mexico. Tezcatlipoca also has a mirror in his forehead with which he sees all human events. God L of the Maya is usually seen smoking a cigar and wearing an owl headdress. These gods, and others like them, hardly suggest the influence of the austere Hebrew God. Certainly we are entitled to some explanation as to why the Israelite beliefs would undergo such a transformation when they arrived in the New World.

An overarching theme in Mesoamerican religions is the cosmic principle of dualism: the unity of opposites. Ometeotl, the god who ruled the Aztec heaven, was bisexual, as was the "Lord and Lady of the Dead," a single deity who reigned in the underworld. Hot and cold, fire and water, life and death, light and dark—these opposing concepts intrigued the Aztec mind much as the concept of *yin* and *yang* permeates Eastern thinking. Perhaps it can be argued that there is some evidence of dualism in ancient Hebrew religion. But a time problem prevents our attributing Mesoamerican religious dualism to the ancient Israelites. We can trace Mesoamerican dualism as far back as 1200 B.C. Archaeologists have found grotesque masks from this period split down the middle to make two different faces. In the 13th century B.C., however, the Children of Israel were being led out of Egypt by Moses, so they could hardly have been introducing religious dualism to the New World. Perhaps the Mormons would argue that the Jaredites brought dualism to the New World in 2800 B.C.

A remarkable 16th-century Mayan document called the *Popol Vuh*, which gives a poetic and imaginative account of "history" from the creation to the Spanish Conquest, is often quoted as evidence of Israelite influence. In its early pages, where the creation is described, the *Popol Vuh* does have a somewhat Biblical flavor. It may be that this similarity is the result of the influence of Spanish clerics, whose favor the Maya eagerly sought. But later in the story, the tone changes dramatically and we are deep in a bloody struggle between the Hero Twins, Hunahpu and

Linda Schele

Pacal after death   World Tree atop the   Chan-Bahlum
                    Quadripartite Monster   before accession
In this drawing of an elaborate stone carving from the Temple of the
Cross in Palenque, in the Yucatan, the Mayan king Chan-Bahlum (right
figure) ascends the throne; the king's deceased father, the former king
Pacal, appears at far left. Between Chan-Bahlum and Pacal stands an
ornate cross-shaped object surmounted by a large supernatural bird, a
Mayan deity. Some modern adventurers have suggested that Jesus, as
well as the ten lost tribes, ended up in the Americas. The Palenque
cross, they claim, is a representation of the cross on which Jesus died.
In fact, this cross represents one of the world trees that, according to
Mayan religious beliefs, stood at each of the four corners and in the center of the universe. The world tree seems to grow out of a monster, which
represents the underworld.

Xbalanque, and the gods of Xibalba, the Mayan underworld,
whom the twins destroy by means of trickery. The story is filled
with gruesome deaths and miraculous reincarnations, none of
which bears any resemblance to the Old Testament.

Both the Maya and the Aztecs engaged in human sacrifice on
a large scale. Some Mesoamerican gods demanded a constant tor-
rent of blood. The Maya perforated their own penises with
stingray spines and beheaded their captives; the Toltecs flung

The Mayan deity Quetzalcoatl appears in all his glory on this page from Lord Kingsborough's nine-volume masterwork, *The Antiquities of Mexico*. Kingsborough believed that Jesus reappeared in the New World in the form of this feathered serpent god.

hapless individuals into *cenotes* or sacred wells; the Aztecs ripped out the hearts of prisoners, sometimes as many as 25,000 at a time. Where in all this is Israelite influence?

As noted earlier, many traditional Mormons also believe that after Jesus was crucified, he was resurrected in the New World as Quetzalcoatl. A similar suggestion was made by Lord Kingsborough. Some Mormons have argued that the "Temple of the Cross" at the Mayan site of Palenque in Chiapas is where Jesus preached to the multitude.

The man (not the god) Quetzalcoatl was a tenth-century A.D. ruler of the Toltecs, named Topiltzin. He supposedly had fair skin and a beard. He has become confused in Indian history with the beneficent ancient god Quetzalcoatl, with whom Topiltzin identified his reign. After losing a civil war, Topiltzin Quetzalcoatl, as he came to be known, left his capital at Tula and migrated with his followers to Chichén Itzá in the Yucatan in 987 A.D. The Aztecs, coming onto the scene a few centuries later, idolized the Toltecs and worshiped Topiltzin Quetzalcoatl as a god. A legend predicted that he would return some day in a boat from the east. When Cortés appeared with his pale skin and beard, he was taken for the returning god and was welcomed by the Aztec leader, Motecuhzoma (much to the local leader's everlasting regret). It is this Toltec king, Topiltzin Quetzalcoatl, who has emerged as Jesus in some Mormon literature.

The so-called cross at the temple of Palenque, where Jesus supposedly preached to the multitude, is actually a representation of one of the four "world trees," a central element of Aztec religion. Each of the four cardinal directions is represented by a tree; another tree stands in the center. The "world tree" concept was widespread in the mythology of North America, Mesoamerica, northern South America, and even on the other side of the Pacific. To the uninitiated, a "world tree" might appear to be a cross. When Cortés landed on the island of Cozumel, off the east coast of Yucatan, he saw "crosses" set up by the Indians, which were undoubtedly world trees. The Spaniards, mightily impressed by these supposed crosses, decided that the apostle Thomas had paid a visit to the New World. (St. Thomas has often been depicted as a wanderer who made great journeys to India and other exotic places.) Father Sahagun, perhaps the most reliable and respected of

Spanish chroniclers of Aztec life, speculated that Topiltzin Quetzalcoatl, with his beard, his pale visage and his reputation for saintliness and good works, was, in fact, the apostle Thomas.

The Mormons took the matter one step further and decided that Topiltzin Quetzalcoatl was the resurrected Jesus.

Yet, whatever we may think of these attempts to locate Jesus and the lost tribes in ancient Mesoamerica, it cannot be denied that the zeal of the search has motivated archaeological discoveries of the greatest importance. And for this we must certainly be grateful.

1. Allen H. Godbey, *The Lost Tribes—A Myth* (New York: KTAV Publishing House, 1974).

2. D. Brent Smith, *The House of Israel and Native Americans* (Provo, UT: Foundation for Ancient Research and Mormon Studies).

3. Thomas Thorowgood, *Jewes in America* (London, 1650).

4. Thomas Stuart Ferguson, *One Fold and One Shepherd* (San Francisco: Books of California, 1958).

5. Michael D. Coe, "Mormons and Archaeology: An Outside View," in *Dialogue: A Journal of Mormon Thought* 8:2 (1973).

6. Coe, *The Maya* (New York: Thames and Hudson, 1984), pp. 43-45.

CHAPTER 7

Lost and Found
Evidence of Tribes Discovered Close to Home

Hershel Shanks

Part of the so-called lost tribes of Israel appears to have been located.

In 721 B.C., the northern kingdom of Israel, composed of ten of the ancient Israelite tribes descended from the sons of Jacob, was conquered and destroyed by Assyria. The Assyrians were among the cruelest people ever to walk across the stage of history. Contemporaneous Assyrian reliefs have been found in which prisoners of the Assyrians are led through the street like dogs, with ropes attached to rings inserted in the septum of the nose. In other reliefs, parading Assyrians hold aloft Hebrew prisoners impaled on Assyrian spears. In accordance with their usual practice, the Assyrians deported much of the upper classes of Israel and settled other peoples in their place. Those who remained intermarried with the newcomers, and out of this amalgamation came the Samaritans. Those who were deported were never heard from again. To history, the tribes who made up the northern kingdom of Israel are known as the ten lost tribes.

However, according to a study by Israeli archaeologist Magen Broshi, many Israelites fled south into the neighboring kingdom of Judah in order to escape the Assyrian onslaught. There they melded with their Hebrew brethren and retained their Hebrew identity.

While all of the evidence has not yet been analyzed, it is becoming increasingly clear that Jerusalem underwent a major expansion during the eighth century B.C. Until that time, Jerusalem was confined to a narrow ridge east of the Tyropoeon Valley. During the eighth century, the city exploded across the valley to the western ridge. By the end of the eighth century, the archaeological evidence indicates, the city had grown to three or four times its former size.

Most of the evidence of this expansion comes from Israeli excavations in the city since 1968. In 1970, Professor Nachman Avigad found a massive wall between 20 and 23 feet wide on the western ridge, which he dates toward the end of the eighth century. Thus, by that time, this section of the city was already enclosed by a wall. Beneath this wall, and therefore earlier than it, Professor Avigad found a structure which may date somewhat earlier in the eighth century, indicating that the western expansion of the city started before the building of the wall there. Excavations west of the wall indicate that, by the end of the eighth century, Jerusalem had extensive suburbs outside the city wall.

Nachman Avigad

This 23-foot-thick wall, which may once have stood as high as 27 feet, was discovered on the western ridge of Jerusalem in 1970. The late archaeologist Nachman Avigad dated the wall to the late eighth century B.C.; the presence of structures beneath (and thus earlier than) the wall indicates that the western expansion of the city began even earlier than this period.

Other excavations on the western ridge of the city (in the area known as David's Citadel, in the Armenian garden and on Mount Zion) have also revealed evidence of initial occupation during this period. All of this makes it clear, according to Broshi, "that Jerusalem at about 700 B.C. had mushroomed, historically speaking, overnight."

According to Broshi, this expansion cannot be explained by natural population growth or by normal economic growth. Moreover, the expansion was relatively sudden rather than gradual. For millennia, the ancient, Jebusite city of Jerusalem had been confined to a small area on the eastern ridge. David's city was likewise limited. Solomon expanded the city northward to include the area of the present Temple Mount. This additional area was used primarily for the Temple, Solomon's royal palace and an administrative area allocated to government buildings. From the death of Solomon to the end of the eighth century B.C.—almost 200 years—the city limits changed very little. Then toward the end of the eighth century the city expanded by a factor of three or four. Broshi estimates the population of the city increased from about 7,500 to 25,000.

Broshi attributes this expansion to two massive waves of immigration. The first he associates with a population flight from the northern kingdom of Israel as a result of the Assyrian conquest in 721 B.C. According to this theory, substantial numbers of the "lost tribes" took up residence in the newly settled parts of Jerusalem.

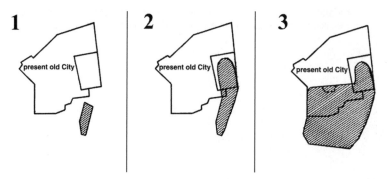

Shading indicates the populated area of Jerusalem during the reigns of (1) King David, c. 1000 B.C., (2) King Solomon, c. 930 B.C. and (3) King Hezekiah, c. 701 B.C.

The second wave of immigration came later in the eighth century, according to Broshi, from Judean territories. As a result of Sennacherib's invasion of Judah at the end of the eighth century, Judah lost considerable territory in the southwestern part of the kingdom to Assyria, which Assyria ceded to the Philistine city-states. Many of the Judeans uprooted by this invasion, Broshi believes, also fled to Jerusalem.

The evidence Broshi cites for the flight of the refugees is not confined to Jerusalem. In 1967 and 1968, a survey conducted by archaeologist Moshe Kochavi of Tel Aviv University revealed that almost half of the settlements in the Judean hills that were occupied during the Judean monarchy were founded during the century before the First Temple was destroyed in 587 B.C. Other scholars have found that numerous sites in other parts of the kingdom of Judah—in the Negev, in the Judean Desert and along the Dead Sea—were first intensively settled in the eighth century. Thus, according to Broshi, the Israelites from the northern kingdom fled not only to Jerusalem but also to numerous other sites in Judah. In this way, large numbers of people from the "lost tribes" of Israel melded into the population of their sister kingdom of Judah. A similar population increase at these sites followed the loss of the western provinces of Judah at the end of the eighth century.[1]

---

1. For further details, see Magen Broshi, "The Expansion of Jerusalem in the Reigns of Hezekiah and Manasseh," *Israel Exploration Journal* 24 (1974), p. 21.

CHAPTER 8

The Tribe of Manasseh
Found in India?

Hershel Shanks, Rivka Gonen, Ronald S. Hendel
and Hillel Halkin

— — —

Introduction

Hershel Shanks

My friend Hillel Halkin recently wrote a book entitled *Across the Sabbath River: In Search of a Lost Tribe of Israel*,[1] in which he claims to have identified descendants of the lost tribe of Manasseh in northeastern India, near the Burmese border. He is an excellent writer, and the book has received rave reviews in such publications as the *New York Times* (which pronounced it "a book that has many delights"), *The New Republic* and the *Wall Street Journal*.

Yet Hillel was not satisfied. He wrote me that "no ordinary reviewer can do justice to my book as a serious scholarly investigation (as opposed to literary entertainment, which it also is)." For this reason, he asked me to consider a review in *Biblical Archaeology Review (BAR)*. The book, he explained, "makes a serious and considered case that should be judged by a professional Bible scholar in a serious and considered way. There's no better or more natural place for this than *BAR*."

I wrote back: "You are taking a risk. Do you know what a Biblical scholar would say?"

Hillel replied: "With all due respect, I took a much greater risk by writing the book in the first place than I am taking by asking you to review it in *BAR*. And I was quite conscious of those risks from the beginning. This is why, out in India, when I first began to suspect that I was wrong in assuming the whole Kuki-Chin-Mizo-ancient-Israel-link-theory to be a modern fabrication, my initial reaction was to groan and say to myself, 'What am I getting myself into?' It would have been much easier—and safer—to write a nice literary book about a people that has deluded itself into thinking that it is a Lost Tribe [rather] than a people of which certain clan groups—in my considered and reconsidered opinion—really are a remnant of such a tribe. I wouldn't have had to worry then about being laughed at or called gullible. I know that.

"Look, Hershel, you know that I'm no nut or enthusiast, and that I am—though, like you, not a scholar with a diploma in Biblical studies—a level-headed and sophisticated person with a good grasp of historical method and historical context. And being such a person, I think I have discovered something significant. I do not think that I have by any means written the last word on the subject, but I do think I have broken ground that now needs to be worked more thoroughly than I possibly could myself…I'm willing to take my chances."

I decided to act on his request. I didn't want a standard book review, but a scholarly assessment of the validity of his thesis. I spoke to Hillel, and we agreed that the issue was not archaeological. It required the attention of an ethnographer and a philologist. Therefore, I asked an Israeli scholar with a specialty in ethnography, Rivka Gonen, to look at the book. Rivka has recently published a book on this topic, so she can usefully compare Halkin's argument with other attempts to identify the lost tribes.[2] Is his claim similar to these, or does it differ in significant respects? Next, I asked Ronald S. Hendel, a leading Hebrew philologist at the University of California at Berkeley, to assess Halkin's philological evidence. Here are their thoughts.

The Cultural View

Rivka Gonen

Having researched the subject of the ten lost tribes of Israel for many years, and having come to the conclusion that the search for them belongs to the realm of metahistory and messianic aspirations, I was hesitant to review Hillel Halkin's book. And yet I was curious to find out why and how Halkin identified tribes living in northeast India and western Burma as remnants of the tribe of Manasseh.

Missionaries of the 19th and early 20th centuries who were active in the mountainous provinces of Mizoram and Manipur in India and across the border in Burma, and who were generally inclined to identify any tribe they encountered with one or another of the ten lost tribes, did not find any clue to possible Israelite descent among the local Kuki-Chin-Mizo peoples. What they did instead was to convert them to Christianity. And yet, sometime in the 1970s, when a Mizo man had recurring dreams of his Israelite descent, his community began to believe in his idea.

Word of this reached Rabbi Eliyahu Avichail of Jerusalem, who has devoted his life to discovering the lost tribes and settling them in the state of Israel. The rabbi visited the region, and when he learned that the people call themselves the Children of Manmasi, he interpreted this as a reference to the tribe of Manasseh. Under Avichail's guidance, the Mizos built synagogues, adopted Jewish prayers, names and customs, and began to insist on migrating to Israel and fully converting to normative Judaism. Indeed, several hundred of them already live in Israel, and there is strong pressure on the rest to do the same.

Halkin accompanied Avichail on his 1998 trip, a trip that he describes in great detail in the first half of the book. He was so intrigued by what he saw and heard that he returned in 1999 to investigate more fully the local beliefs, customs, rituals and memories, accounts of which make up the second part of the book. At the end of a long series of interviews with many people from the Mizo and neighboring tribes, including people who traveled from Burma to tell him their stories, Halkin was left with a handful of "clues." It is on this dubious foundation that he builds a fascinating tale of how members of the Israelite tribe of Manasseh migrated to northeast India.

The first of these clues is the very name by which the Hualngo and Hmar peoples call themselves: "sons of Manmasi." Notwithstanding the vague similarity between "Manmasi" and "Manasseh," surely the former can be interpreted many other ways. I do not know any of the languages spoken in the region, or in East Asia in general, so I cannot offer an alternative explanation; but I am reminded of the case of the "British Israelites," a Victorian group that claimed the British were descended from the lost tribes, and believed the term "British" derived from *berit 'ish*, "covenant of man" in Hebrew.

Another Mizo term that Halkin discusses is *Sangah Meichol*, also pronounced Sangametsal, a wildcat that, in local folklore, drove the people out of their land. Halkin identifies *Sangah Meichol* with the Assyrian King Shalmaneser V (726–722 B.C.E.), who, he claims, exiled the tribe of Manasseh from Israel. His linguistic derivation is based on shared consonant sounds—*l*, *m* and *n*. Even if such a derivation is possible, the historical fact is that the Transjordanian part of the tribe of Manasseh, the part on which Halkin focuses, was exiled not by Shalmaneser but by Tiglath-pileser III in 733–732 B.C.E. When Shalmaneser V besieged Samaria and his son Sargon exiled its inhabitants in 721 B.C.E., Transjordanian Manasseh had already been in exile for more than ten years.

Halkin detects other clues in the tribes' folklore and customs. The Kuki and Mizo peoples "remembered" the crossing of the Red Sea and sang songs about it. But the crossing of a dangerous body of water does not necessarily correspond to the Biblical crossing of the Red (or Reed) Sea. That event in the Bible was indeed momentous, but surely less so than the receiving of the Law at Mt. Sinai, an event that is not reflected in these tribes' traditions. The chief god of the tribes is known as *Pathen*, but his secret name is *Za* or *Ya*, which Halkin believes stems from the name of the Israelite God, *Yahweh*. However, the tribes of Israel were idol-worshipers, as is mentioned time and again in the Bible. Why would the lost tribes remember the name of a god they did not worship?

Circumcision is another important issue for Halkin. It has always been regarded as a "sure" marker of the lost tribes—despite the fact that all tribes living along the Nile, and all Muslims, follow this custom. Hence the Zulu, who used to practice circumcision, were declared Israelites by the first missionaries who encountered them. Similarly, lost-tribe-seekers in South America observed that some Native American tribes performed circumcision and conferred upon them an Israelite heritage.

Dietary practices, if they are similar to those of the Jews, are also seized upon as "evidence" by most seekers of the lost tribes. Yes, the Mizos refrain from eating pork, but so do the Zulus and the Navajo people of the southwestern United States. As for festive customs, North American tribes have been said to celebrate a festival similar to the Jewish Feast of the First Fruit (*Shavuot*, or Pentecost), and other groups have been reported to perform a ritual akin to the sacrifice of the Passover lamb.

It is to Halkin's credit that he does not get carried away with his story. After all his interviews and ethnographic research, he concludes that, at most, perhaps a tiny group—one family—of hypothetical Transjordanian Manassehites traveled the long and hazardous route from Assyria to their present home. (This "historical" reconstruction is gleaned from tribal songs that mention certain place-names on the supposed route.) Indeed, historians and anthropologists accept that the hill tribes in question did originate elsewhere, in Tibet or China. Halkin suggests that this handful of wandering Transjordanian Manassehites kept alive some distant memory of Israelite practices. For some reason he does not explain, the neighboring communities adopted their traditions, which then developed into the belief that they all were descended from the tribe of Manasseh.

Halkin's long, minutely detailed descriptions of people, places, conversations, journeys, meals and the like make *Across the Sabbath River* somewhat cumbersome. One eventually loses track of who is who and who did what and where. And because the book has no index, there is no way to return to a passage of special interest. But most important of all, Halkin has failed to prove his case.

The Linguistic View

Ronald S. Hendel

Hillel Halkin recounts some relatively recent history of the Mizo people of northeast India and western Burma. They came under British rule in 1892; after Anglican missionaries arrived in 1894, they began to convert to Christianity, becoming almost entirely Christianized by the dawn of Indian independence in 1947. Then, in the early 1950s, a Mizo man named Chala had a vision. As Halkin relates, "An angel revealed to him that the Mizo people were the descendants of Israelites and should return to their ancestral land." Many of these people are now hoping to be airlifted to Israel.

Halkin believes that these people are descended from the lost tribes of Israel. He places a great deal of weight on the following linguistic equations. As shown below, the first half of each equation is the Mizo word or phrase and its meaning; the second half is Halkin's proposed ancient Hebrew (or Greek) original.

- *Sangah meichol* ("long-tailed wildcat," a trickster in Mizo folklore) = Shalmaneser (king of Assyria)
- *shelah* ("say it again") = *selah* (obscure Hebrew word in the book of Psalms)
- *aborizah* ("the end," or a magical word) = *ha-borey Yah* ("God the creator")
- *Manmasi* (eponymous tribal ancestor) = Menashe (the Israelite tribe of Manasseh)
- *Gelet* (tribal ancestor) = *Gil'ad* (the Israelite region of Gilead)
- *akuptan* (a place?) = *Aigyptos* (Greek word for "Egypt")

From the standpoint of Hebrew linguistics, these equations are wholly imaginary. As a basis for ethnographic history, they have no more merit than the equation of the English word "British" with *berit 'ish* (Hebrew for "covenant of man"), which Rivka Gonen notes was once advanced as proof that the British were descended from the lost tribes of

Israel. Halkin's linguistic equations are the result of his random association of sounds. He states that he is "107 percent certain" that these people are descended from the lost tribes of Israel. I would suggest that his grasp of linguistics is as reliable as his math.

The most ludicrous of these derivations is Mizo *akuptan* = *Aigyptos*, the Greek word for "Egypt." Halkin surmises that the lost tribes picked up *Aigyptos* from Greek soldiers in ancient Bactria (northern Afghanistan). But he offers no real reason to think that *akuptan* refers to Egypt anyway.

As for the second most ludicrous equation, it's a toss-up. One candidate is Mizo *aborizah* = *ha-borey Yah*. The divine title *ha-borey* ("the creator") is not Biblical Hebrew but rabbinic, and therefore it could not have been known to the lost tribes. Tied for second place is Mizo *Sangah meichol* (long-tailed wildcat) = Shalmaneser, which strikes me as either wishful thinking or sheer baloney.

As far as Hebrew linguistics goes, there is no merit whatever in Halkin's thesis.

Lost Tribes in India: Halkin Responds to His Critics

Hillel Halkin

As Hershel Shanks pointed out in his introductory remarks to the two reviews of my book *Across the Sabbath River*, I didn't send the book to *BAR* in the hope of getting another "good" review. *Across the Sabbath River* had enough good reviews, and in sufficiently prestigious places, to satisfy me. But these reviews were literary ones, and because the book, besides telling an adventure story, argues a case that the best literary reviewer is not fully equipped to assess, it was important for me to bring it to the attention of the scholarly community, as well. I knew, as Hershel observed, that I was taking a risk, since scholars, often with good reason, tend to be suspicious of, and condescending toward, non-scholars intruding on their fields. Yet it was a risk I felt I needed to take.

The reason for this was simple. The old, pre-Christian religious traditions of segments of the Kuki-Chin-Mizo people of the northeastern Indian states of Mizoram and Manipur that point to a link with ancient Israel can be attested today only by a small number of elderly individuals who still remember them and are part of a dying generation. Within a few years, many of these people will be gone; in a decade or two, all will be. If scholars—Biblical historians, linguists, anthropologists, ethnographers—are going to investigate the many amazing and detailed parallels between these traditions and Biblical religion, and to try to determine what significance they may have, they will have to act quickly, because otherwise there will be little left to investigate. I had hoped—wrongly—that a review in *BAR* might help to arouse the scholarly interest needed to get such a process going.

I was well aware in writing *Across the Sabbath River* that the initial scholarly reaction to its conclusion that certain Kuki-Chin-Mizo clan groups have a historical connection to the Biblical tribe of Manasseh would be to consign it automatically to the vast body of lunatic literature on the "Lost Tribes" of Israel, and I went to great lengths to explain why this would be a mistake. I regret that Rivka Gonen and Ronald Hendel, in their reviews in *BAR*, did not comment on these lengths and do not appear even to have noticed them. But neither of them, I must say, seems to have done more than leaf quickly through *Across the Sabbath River* with his or her mind already made up. In all of their superciliously dismissive criticisms, there is not a single one that I do not anticipate and deal with fully in the book—yet to read their reviews, you would think I was simply another "Lost-Tribe" crank not worth wasting their time on.

This is unfortunate, not because of any injury done to me, but because of the injury done to a fascinating cultural and historical mystery that is begging for scholarly attention. I can only appeal to those scholars who have the curiosity and desire to explore that Ms. Gonen and Mr. Hendel sorely lack to read

Across the Sabbath River and decide for themselves. It would be a great shame if we forever lost the chance to prove or disprove the most persuasive claim for a "Lost-Tribe" past that has ever been put forth for any people on earth, and to learn what we can from it should it turn out to be true.

---

1. Hillel Halkin, *Across the Sabbath River: In Search of a Lost Tribe of Israel* (New York: Houghton Mifflin, 2002).

2. Rivka Gonen, *The Quest for the Ten Lost Tribes of Israel* (Northvale, NJ: Aronson, 2002).

"They shall make an Ark of acacia wood; it shall be two and a half cubits long, a cubit and a half wide, and a cubit and a half high. You shall overlay it with pure gold, inside and outside you shall overlay it, and you shall make a molding of gold upon it all around. You shall cast four rings of gold for it and put them on its four feet, two rings on the one side of it, and two rings on the other side. You shall make poles of acacia wood, and overlay them with gold. And you shall put the poles into the rings on the sides of the Ark, by which to carry the Ark. The poles shall remain in the rings of the Ark, they shall not be taken from it. You shall put into the Ark the Covenant that I shall give you.

"Then you shall make a mercy seat of pure gold; two cubits and a half shall be its length, and a cubit and a half its width. You shall make two cherubim of gold; you shall make them of hammered work, at the two ends of the mercy seat ... There I will meet with you, and from above the mercy seat, from between the two cherubim that are on the Ark of the Covenant I will deliver to you all my commands for the Israelites."

(Exodus 25:10-18,22)

Part V

THE ARK OF THE COVENANT

The Israelites carefully transported the sacred Ark, designed by God to hold the Ten Commandments, from Mt. Sinai through the Wilderness, to Canaan and eventually to Jerusalem, where King Solomon installed it with great ceremony in the Temple he had built. And there it remained—but for how long?

By 586 B.C., when the Babylonians destroyed Jerusalem and its Temple, and exiled the Jews to Babylon, the Ark may have already been lost. It is conspicuously absent from the detailed list of treasures that the Babylonians removed from the Temple. According to the Book of Kings, the Babylonian king Nebuchadnezzar "carried off all the treasures of the House of the Lord [the Temple]; he cut in pieces all the vessels of gold in the Temple ... They took away the pots, the shovels, the snuffers, the dishes for incense, and all the bronze vessels used in the Temple service, as well as the firepans and the basins. What was made of gold the captain of the guard took away for the gold, and what was made of silver, for the silver" (1 Kings 24:13,14-15). Nor is the Ark listed among the thousands of Temple vessels that the prophet Ezra tells us the Jews brought back to Jerusalem when the Persian king Cyrus ended the Exile in 538 B.C. (Ezra 1:9). Just as the prophet Jeremiah had predicted, the day had arrived when the Ark of the Covenant was no longer "remembered, or missed" (Jeremiah 3:16).

The seeming disappearance of this most sacred relic is one of the most famous of the many Biblical mysteries. Yet, one of the oldest extrabiblical traditions about the Ark, described by Ephraim Isaac in the following chapter, suggests that it may never have been lost at all; rather, it may be hidden away in a quiet chapel in the sacred city of Axum, Ethiopia. This ancient Ethiopian tradition has recently been popularized by British journalist Graham Hancock, who has also suggested the Ark traveled to Ethiopia by way of Elephantine Island, in Egypt—a contention discounted by Bezalel Porten in Chapter 10.

CHAPTER 9

From Israel to Ethiopia
The Journey of the Ark

Ephraim Isaac

———————

Ever since the movie *Raiders of the Lost Ark* came out, hardly a year passes without someone claiming to have found the Ark of the Covenant. Yet, according to a very well-known Ethiopian tradition, the Ark never did disappear but was instead sent to Ethiopia in the time of King Solomon. The ancient tradition has received much attention lately as Graham Hancock, a much-published British journalist formerly with *The Economist*, recently claimed that he had located the Ark of the Covenant in "a secluded sanctuary chapel" in Axum, Ethiopia.

As described in the Book of Exodus, the Ark is a wooden chest measuring 4 feet, 2 inches (2.5 cubits) long; 2 feet, 6 inches (1.5 cubits) wide; and 2 feet, 6 inches (1.5 cubits) high. Two of the most skilled Israelite craftsmen fashioned the Ark out of *shittim*, or acacia wood, overlaid with gold inside and outside. A golden crown and two cherubs facing each other decorated the top. It was covered by a pure gold cloth called *kaporet*. During processions, the Ark was carried by staves inserted into four golden rings at the bottom corners (Exodus 25:10–22, 37:1–9).

The Ark is the most holy and powerful object described in the Hebrew Bible. First mentioned in Exodus 25:10 as the repository of the Tablets of the Law given to Moses upon Mt. Sinai, it symbolized the divine presence in Israel. Human beings were strictly forbidden to touch or even to gaze upon it (Leviticus 16:2; Numbers 4:15,19,20). Many great deeds were performed before it. Perhaps most famously, the walls of Jericho fell after the Ark was carried around the city seven times (Joshua 6:12–20).

The Ark accompanied the Israelites on their journey from Sinai and throughout the entire period of the conquest of Canaan. It was first kept at Shiloh (Joshua 18:1; 1 Samuel 3:3), and it accompanied the Israelite army into battles, falling once into the hands of the Philistines near Eben-Ezer (1 Samuel 4, 14:18). When Shiloh was destroyed (Psalms 78:59–67; Jeremiah 26:6–9), the Ark was kept at Beth-Shemesh until a plague necessitated its transfer to Abinadab's house on the hill in Kiriath-Jearim (1 Samuel 7:1). It was then placed in the house of Obed-Edom the Gittite for three months, after which it was brought to Jerusalem and kept in a special tent (2 Samuel 6:2–17). Finally the Ark came to rest in a special permanent place in the innermost sanctuary, the Holy of Holies, of the Temple built by Solomon (1 Kings 8:6). Thereafter, there is no mention of the Ark being carried to war or festivals.

Some scholars—basing their views on the prophet Jeremiah's description of a day when the Ark "shall not come to mind, or be remembered, or missed" (Jeremiah 3:16), and on the absence of the Ark from the lists of vessels carried into and brought back from the Exile in Babylon—suggest that the Ark was no longer in the Temple at the time of its destruction by the Babylonians in 586 B.C.E. Furthermore, the Temple built by the returned exiles does not seem to have possessed the Ark (Babylonian Talmud, *Yoma* 5:2). According to another passage in the Talmud, the Ark had been hidden by King Josiah "in its place," or beneath the "woodshed" (*Shekalim* 6:1–2; *Yoma* 53b–54a). Another source, 2 Maccabees 2:1–7, says Jeremiah hid the Ark on Mount Nebo. The many modern attempts to explain the disappearance or whereabouts of the Ark have been to no avail.

The Ethiopian tradition of the Ark's removal and present location is recorded in the *Kebra Nagast,* a highly valued Ethiopic literary work whose origin (Ethiopic, Jewish, Coptic or Arabic?) and date of composition (sometime between the sixth and ninth century C.E., and revised in the fourteenth century) are matters of some scholarly dispute. This work claims that the Ark of the Covenant, called *tabot* in Ge'ez (classical Ethiopic), was brought from Jerusalem to Ethiopia by the Queen of Sheba's alleged son by Solomon—Ibn-al-Hakim (Dawit), known popularly as Menelik. According to the same tradition, the Jewish religion was also introduced to Ethiopia at this time. The word *tabot* is derived from the Jewish Aramaic term *tebuta,* also related to Hebrew *tebah,* meaning "ark" or "box."

Many factors suggest that Christianity came to Ethiopia in the early centuries of the Common Era. According to Ethiopian church tradition, the Ethiopian eunuch mentioned in Acts 8:26–39 brought Christianity to the country. Scholars, however, date its origin to about 330 C.E., when the royal family was converted to Christianity by a Syrian monk named Frumentius.

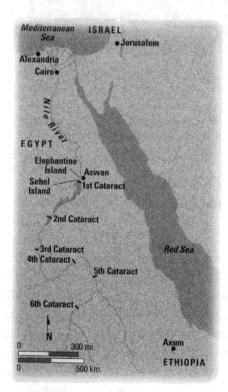

Tradition also holds that when Christianity came to Ethiopia, half of the population was Jewish and that most of these Jews converted to Christianity. Literary, linguistic, archaeological and historical sources confirm that there were Jews and Jewish converts in Ethiopia in the early Christian centuries. It was probably these Jews and Jewish converts who were responsible for the strong Jewish molding of Ethiopian culture, including the incorporation of the *tabot* into the ritual of the Ethiopian church.

This photo from about 1905 shows a priest (front right) in Axum, Ethiopia, balancing on his head a chest containing a replica of the Ark of the Covenant. In the background is the Church of Mary Zion, where, according to ancient Ethiopic tradition, Solomon's son Menelik deposited the original Ark, the elaborate container for the Ten Commandments that God ordered Moses to construct.

The *tabot* is the most holy object of the Ethiopian church. Its sanctity, function and centrality in the ritual of the Ethiopian church is the same as that of the Ark in ancient Israel. But whereas the Ark was carried on shoulders at ceremonies in ancient Israel (except once when it was conveyed in a cart [2 Samuel 6:3]), the *tabot* is carried on the heads of officiating priests during religious processions. The priests march with dignity a step at a time, followed by a company of singing, dancing and clapping priests and deacons who beat drums and praying sticks and shake *sistra* (sacred rattles). The solemn congregation, kept at some distance, follows quietly and serenely—except for occasional bursts into ululation. The veneration of the *tabot* has been compared by some scholars to David and the people singing and dancing around the Ark as it was brought to Jerusalem (2 Samuel 6:5,14–16).

Ethiopian tradition holds that the original Israelite Ark is still lying in the famous, ancient Church of Mary Zion in Axum. Guarded by a monk who devotes his life to the task, it is off limits to all persons, including kings and bishops. Its replicas, however, are found in all Ethiopian churches and monasteries. No one is supposed to see or touch even these replicas, let alone the original Ark. No church is fit for worship unless a copy of the Ark is installed in it, and no service is considered sacred without its presence. The tradition probably goes back to the early days, if not to the beginning, of the Ethiopian church. It should be noted, however, that Ethiopian Jews also adhere to the tradition of the Ark coming to Ethiopia in the days of King Solomon and the Queen of Sheba and of the existence of Jews in pre-Christian Ethiopia. They claim with good reason that, even though they lost political power to the Christians, they are the true descendants and heirs of those ancient Jews.

The Armenian writer Abu Salih is one of several medieval commentators who, in the early 13th century, noted the Ark's importance in the Ethiopian church. He gave the following very accurate description of the Ark's role in the church:

> The Abyssinians [Ethiopians] possess also the Ark of the Covenant, in which are the two tables of stone, inscribed by the Finger of God with the commandments which he ordained for the children of Israel. The Ark of the Covenant is placed upon the altar, but is not so wide as the altar; it is as high as the knee of a man, and is overlaid with gold; and upon its upper cover there are crosses of gold; and there are five precious stones upon it, one at each of the four corners, and one in the middle. The liturgy is celebrated upon the Ark four times in the year, within the palace of the king; and a canopy is spread over it when it is taken out from its own church to the church which is in the palace of the king; namely on the feast of the great Nativity, on the feast of the glorious Baptism, on the feast of the holy Resurrection, and on the feast of the illuminating Cross. And the Ark is attended and carried by a large number of Israelites descended from the family of the prophet David.[1]

Almost all of these words, recorded about 800 years before Hancock, could have been written in 1993. They describe succinctly the practices prevalent in the Ethiopian church to this very day, albeit with replicas substituted for the original Ark. Over the past 400 years, numerous scholars who have written about Ethiopia or about the Jewish component of Ethiopian culture have underlined the significance of the Ark in the Ethiopian church, for it is impossible to write about that country without referring to the centrality of the Ark in its Christian tradition.[2]

Journalist Graham Hancock, in his popular book *The Sign and the Seal*, relies on this tradition in claiming that the Ark is not "in Israel beneath the Temple Mount (as many believe), but in the highlands of war-torn Ethiopia in a secluded sanctuary chapel at the heart of the ancient and sacred city of Axum. There, guarded by a secretive brotherhood of monks, it forms the centerpiece of a pervasive cult which incorporates elements of early Judaism, of Christianity, and of paganism in arcane rituals and in bizarre and archaic ceremonies that are found nowhere else in the world."[3]

It is evident to anyone knowledgeable in the literature and history of Ethiopian Christianity that this claim contains little that is new. Hancock does, however, introduce a couple new but controversial ideas in his book. Contrary to the accepted Ethiopian tradition (that Menelik brought the Ark to Dabra Makidda, in Ethiopia, the capital of the Queen of Sheba, during Solomon's reign), Hancock suggests that the Ark arrived in Ethiopia in the fifth century B.C.E., 500 years after the Queen of Sheba's famous visit to Jerusalem. Moreover, he says that it did not go directly to Axum from Jerusalem, but from a Jewish temple on Elephantine Island in Egypt, via another Jewish temple on Lake Tana, the source of the Blue Nile.

These suggestions are interesting, but none of them can be proven one way or another. Further, many scholars would dispute them vehemently, arguing that there is no factual evidence to demonstrate such historical movements or connections between the Jewish communities of Elephantine Island and Ethiopia.

Hancock also claims that he discovered evidence of a series of covert quests for the sacred relic in Ethiopia since the time of the Crusades. He asserts that in 1185 the Templars located the Ark in Ethiopia, but that they were unable to return it to Jerusalem. Subsequently, Portuguese adventurers such as Prince Henry the Navigator and Christopher de Gama (Vasco da Gama's son), all belonging to the Order of Christ (formed in Portugal to shelter fugitive Templars in the early 14th century), trailed the Ark. More recently, a shadowy group of Freemasons, whose traditions supposedly descend directly from the Templars, have renewed the quest with hopes of revealing the Ark to the world.

Hancock also hypothesizes that the Holy Grail legend was invented in the 12th century by the writers Chrétien de Troyes and Wolfram von Eschenbach (also associated with the Templars) as an occult symbol for the real and historical Ark in literary allegories that describe real-life quests for the Ark of the Covenant. Thus, the location of the Ark has been transmitted to succeeding generations in the enigmatic Grail literature.

These claims are equally fascinating, but likewise condemned by scholars, who believe that Hancock's ideas are fanciful and not supported by a shred of evidence.

Some of my colleagues have labeled the book in which Hancock presents his ideas "trash," "an adventure story," "a sensational best-seller story," a "publicity-seeking gimmick" and the like.[4] That is not only unkind, but also unfair and inaccurate. Hancock has revived an old debate concerning a most significant religious object. He has resuscitated interest in an unsolved mystery and thrown new light upon it. He has generated new interest in Ethiopia, an ancient and fascinating land. If for no other reasons, the author deserves praise for these accomplishments.

While Hancock's book is definitely not trash, his claim that he has discovered the Ark of the Covenant is an exaggeration. He has not done that. What he has done is to publicize an ancient Ethiopian claim. For centuries, the Ethiopians have had a firm belief that they possess the Ark of the Covenant. As alluded to above, this belief has not escaped the attention of a single scholar of note who has dealt with the history and culture of Ethiopia.

Certain scholarly colleagues of mine also say that Hancock is not qualified to deal with a subject that requires years of study of many ancient languages and history. Because he has not done so, they say, his work is full of errors. This judgment is not totally fair either. Hancock has done a great deal of research, albeit from secondary sources (as many modern social scientists do) rather than from primary sources (as scholars in our field do). True, he has relied a lot on oral information gathered from interviews with scholars in Israel and Ethiopia and on impressions of places that he has visited, but he has also read many important works that deal with the subject. In addition, Hancock writes well and communicates his ideas provocatively.

More importantly, he has tried to solve a historical puzzle by putting together, in a rather creative way, all the information available to him. Of course, whether his solution adequately addresses the problem is another matter. Indeed, his lack of the knowledge of the languages and his narrow understanding of the scholarly debate have led him to make hasty, albeit interesting, judgments. Ironically, however, it is his lack of the necessary scholarly tools that makes Hancock an original thinker!

As a scholar of both Jewish and Ethiopian literatures and cultures, I am fully aware of the complexities of the issues with which this book deals. For example, all Christians have some form of an altar. Is the Ethiopian Ark an ancient altar, as at least one scholar once suggested? Or is the Ethiopian Ark some sort of ancient Semitic ritual object? And, if so, is it the original Israelite Ark of the Covenant? These questions await more serious scholarly research. In the meantime, we have to respect the Ethiopian claims, so sacred, weighty and ancient, and not make a wild guess as to the true nature of the artifact that now rests in Axum.

---

1. B.T.A. Evetts, transl. and ed., *Abu Salih: Churches and Monasteries of Egypt and Some Neighboring Countries* (Oxford, 1895), pp. 105b, 106a. The Arabic text appears on p. 133.

2. See, for example, Ephraim Isaac, "An Obscure Component in Ethiopian Church History," *Le Museon* 85 (1972), pp. 225–258; Isaac, *A Text-Critical Introduction to Mashafa Berhan* (Leiden: E.J. Brill, 1973), pp. 109, 116, 118, etc.; E. Hammerschmidt, "Jewish Elements in the Cult of the Ethiopian Church," *Journal of Ethiopian Studies* (1965), pp. 1–12; E. Ullendorff, *Ethiopia and the Bible* (Oxford: The British Academy/Oxford Univ. Press, 1968), pp. 82–87; M. Rodinson, "Sur la question des influences juives en Ethiopie," *Journal of Semitic Studies* 9 (1964), pp. 11–19; H. Ludolf, *Commentarius ad suam Historiam Aethiopicam* (Frankfort: 1961); J.S. Trimmingham, *Islam in Ethiopia* (London: Oxford, 1952); C. Rathjens, *Die Juden in Abessinien* (Hamburg, 1921), p. 48; H.M. Hyatt, *The Church of Abyssinia* (London, 1928), p. 169ff. T. Bent, *The Sacred City of the Ethiopians* (London, 1893), p. 55ff.

3. Graham Hancock, *The Sign and the Seal: The Quest for the Lost Ark of the Covenant* (New York: Crown, 1992).

4. Scholars have shunned a public discussion of the book on the grounds that it is not a scholarly work. A presentation by Hancock planned for the University of Toronto was abruptly canceled when, according to reports, some scholars vehemently opposed it.

Chapter 10

From Jerusalem to Egypt
Did the Ark Stop at Elephantine?

Bezalel Porten

⎯⎯➤◆⎯⎯

Was the Ark of the Covenant taken from Solomon's Temple in Jerusalem during the reign of King Manasseh in the seventh century B.C.E. to an island called Elephantine in the Nile River? Was it housed there in a Jewish temple much like the one King Solomon built?

These are the contentions of Graham Hancock in his bestseller, *The Sign and the Seal: The Quest for the Lost Ark of the Covenant.*[1] According to Hancock, more than two centuries later the Ark of the Covenant moved on from Elephantine on the Nile to Ethiopia, where it still resides in a "secluded sanctuary chapel" in Axum.[2]

A former writer for the London *Economist*, Hancock is an excellent researcher who understands what he reads. His contention about the Ark's temporary stop at Elephantine, therefore, bears looking at. If it proves to be incorrect, or overly speculative, at least we will learn a lot about a fascinating Egyptian island and the cache of ancient Aramaic texts discovered there.

One item is not speculative, however. There was a Jewish temple on Elephantine in the sixth and fifth centuries B.C.E.,

Sailboats ply the Nile waters near Elephantine Island. In the distance lies the western shore of the Nile, with the domed mausoleum of the Aga Khan. According to a hoard of Aramaic papyri discovered in Egypt at the turn of the last century, a Jewish temple stood on the southern tip of Elephantine Island during the sixth and fifth centuries B.C.E. No archaeological remains have been uncovered.

where sacrifices, including animal sacrifices, were offered. Regardless of what else may be said of Hancock's arguments, this much is factual.

We know this not because archaeologists have dug up remnants of the Jewish temple on the island, but because it is referred to in an extraordinary hoard of documents known as the Elephantine papyri. The saga of their discovery reads almost like a 19th-century novel. It begins with a character named Charles Edwin Wilbour, an American journalist who managed the *New York Transcript*, a major daily. Exactly why, at the age of 38, he left for permanent exile, we will probably never know. It could have had something to do with a city printing contract steered his way by Boss Tweed; trouble may have been in the wind. In any event, in 1874 Wilbour left for Paris, where he studied Egyptology with the great Gaston Maspero. Maspero called Wilbour "the friendliest Yankee I know." The American Egyptologist John A. Wilson described Wilbour as "a fine figure of a man, large, broad-shouldered, with a fine brow, a well-sculptured nose, and that wonderful white bib of a beard reaching down to the second button of his waistcoat."[3] By the late 1880s, Wilbour was a regular visitor to Egypt, with his own sailing *dahabiyeh* (a large lateen-rigged house-boat popular on the Nile), named "Seven Hathors" after Egyptian goddesses of fortune. Each winter he would escape the Paris cold to ply the Nile, visiting excavations, copying inscriptions and collecting fine antiquities for modest prices. Wilbour obtained some of his choicest finds around the First Cataract of the Nile at Aswan, opposite the island of Elephantine.[4] One text, published by Maspero, describes how the Twelfth Dynasty pharaoh Sesostris I (c. 1971–1928 B.C.E.) cut a channel 260 feet long, 34 feet wide and nearly 26 feet deep through the Nile cataract above Elephantine.

Wilbour also discovered the famous "Famine Stela" on the island of Sehel at the First Cataract. Written in the second century B.C.E., it tells how the Third Dynasty king Djoser assigned the ram-god Khnum, the god of Elephantine, a stretch of land to relieve a seven-year famine. The echo of the Joseph narrative in Genesis is evident.

In early 1893, Wilbour acquired some papyri from "3 separate women at different times,"[5] according to his notebook entries for January and February of that year. Also included in the cache were fragments in an envelope on which he wrote, "Is not this authentic Phenician [sic]?" Wilbour showed the fragments to a distinguished Biblical scholar, the Reverend A.H. Sayce, who had often traveled with Wilbour; Sayce correctly identified the piece as Aramaic. Wilbour died in 1896 without having done anything with the hoard he had purchased from the "3 separate women." After his death, it was shipped back to the States in a trunk, along with his other finds. That trunk rested in a New York warehouse until the death of his daughter Theodora in 1947 and then went to the Egyptian Department of the Brooklyn Museum. Only at that time, after the finds had lain unexamined for more than 50 years, did scholars learn that Wilbour had acquired the first Elephantine papyri—which included the fragments in the envelope that Sayce had identified as Aramaic.[6] (Aramaic is akin to Hebrew, one of a number of northwestern Semitic languages. It was the language of Aram [Syria] and the *lingua franca* of the Assyrian and Persian empires.)

The next acquisition of an Elephantine papyrus was made by Sayce himself. A bachelor and Oxford professor, Sayce also regularly

New York journalist and amateur Egyptologist Charles Edwin Wilbour (left) visited Egypt regularly in the 1880s, where he sailed along the Nile in his *dahabiyeh* (below), or house-boat, named "Seven Hathors" after Egyptian goddesses of fortune. In Egypt, Wilbour collected several ancient papyri, which, after his death, were packed in tin biscuit boxes, placed in the bottom of a trunk and shipped to a New York warehouse. There they remained until 1947, when Wilbour's daughter bequeathed them to the Brooklyn Museum. Only then did scholars realize that Wilbour had unwittingly acquired the first of the Elephantine papyri.

Brooklyn Museum/Egyptian Department

sailed the Nile in his own *dahabiyeh*. While docked at Elephantine in early 1901, he was led by what he called his "lucky star" to an ancient mound where some natives were digging *sebakh*, the local nitrate-rich fertilizer. Sayce could see some papyrus fragments and ostraca (inscribed potsherds) mixed with the fertilizer, which he proceeded to "rescue" from what he felt would have been certain oblivion. Upon his return to Oxford, he presented them to the Bodleian Library. They turned out to be three rolls that actually constituted a single Aramaic papyrus. This manuscript was published in 1903 by Sir Arthur Ernest Cowley, who characterized it as "the longest and most continuous text of the kind hitherto published." It was a loan contract involving at least one Jew, dating to the fifth century B.C.E.

The great acquisition, however, was made in 1904 when two British philanthropists, Lady William Cecil and Mr. (later Sir) Robert Ludwig Mond, separately acquired a total of 10 rolls. Lady Cecil and Mond had intended to ship the documents to a British institution, but Howard Carter, the Englishman who was then serving as inspector general of the Service des Antiquités de l'Égypte, prevailed upon them to turn the texts over to the Egyptian Museum in Cairo. One papyrus, however, did find its way into the Bodleian Library at Oxford.

The Cecil-Mond papyri were published in record time (1906) and in large folio format by Sayce and Cowley. The two scholars had been given two versions of the findspot of the papyri—one on Elephantine and the other at Aswan. In their publication, Sayce wrote, "That this latter was the true story [i.e., Aswan] seems to admit little doubt." This was a critical error. If Sayce had searched further at Elephantine, he might well have succeeded in discovering more texts.

In 1904 natives showed the findspot on Elephantine to Otto Rubensohn of the Königlichen (today Staatlichen) Museen in Berlin. Rubensohn soon organized an archaeological expedition to the site. There, on New Year's Day in 1907, he uncovered, just below the surface, three major documents relating to a Jewish temple at Elephantine. The texts were promptly forwarded to Berlin, where they were unrolled by the master conservator, Hugo Ibscher, and their contents were promptly published by Eduard Sachau. Rubensohn and his colleague and successor Friedrich Zucker then went on to discover many more Aramaic papyri at the site, including 19 letters, 18 contracts, 9 lists and accounts, a copy of the Behistun (alternatively, Bisitun) inscription of Darius the Great (522–486 B.C.E.), a 14-column work of ethical and wisdom literature known as the Words of Ahiqar, as well as numerous fragments and inscriptions on potsherds, wood and stone. The whole collection was brought out in 1911 in large format, with excellent commentary by Sachau.[7]

Wilbour's dozen rolls and several fragments that were locked in a trunk in a New York warehouse for half a century were published by Emil Kraeling after finally being opened. Most of these documents constituted the family archive of a local man named Anani, to be discussed later. It took Kraeling, who published the lot in 1953, about the same time it took Sachau to publish the much larger German lot nearly a half century earlier.

Both archives contain several house conveyances that mark property boundaries by delineating the four adjacent buildings. One building bordering several houses was an 'egora. In the Targum, the Aramaic translation of the Bible, the word refers to an open-air altar. But that is hardly what the word meant in a fifth-century B.C.E. Jewish neighborhood on Elephantine. One scholar suggested it might be a synagogue. It turned out not to be a synagogue or an open-air sanctuary, but a cedar-roofed Jewish temple in which animal sacrifices were offered.

In 1961, with the help of some of the house dimensions that were given, I was able to come up with a reconstruction of the temple. Oriented toward Jerusalem, the temple measured 60 cubits long and 20 cubits wide—the same dimensions as Solomon's Temple (1 Kings 6:2).

This was the Elephantine temple where—according to Graham Hancock—the Ark of the Covenant from Solomon's Temple was taken before moving on to Axum, where it supposedly remains to this day.

The claim that the Ark was taken to Ethiopia is an old one, and, as Ephraim Isaac notes in the previous chapter, in this respect Hancock presents "little that is new." Contrary to the Ethiopian tradition, however, Hancock argues that the Ark went first to Elephantine in Egypt, arriving in Ethiopia only in the fifth century B.C.E.

The mystery of the Ark stems from the silence of the Bible after we are told that it was placed in the Holy of Holies of Solomon's Temple (1 Kings 8:6). Nowhere in the Bible, neither in the account of the Babylonian destruction of the Temple in 587/6 B.C.E. (2 Kings 25), nor anywhere else, is there an indication of the fate of the Ark. Over the years, its curious disappearance has given rise to a great deal of speculation.

Dear Jerusalem: Priests Petition to Rebuild Their Temple

In this draft letter dated November 25, 407 B.C.E., Jedaniah, leader of Elephantine's Jewish community, and his priestly colleagues ask Bagohi, the governor of the Persian province of Judah, to intercede on their behalf for the rebuilding of their temple:

To our lord Bagavahya governor of Judah, your servants Jedaniah and his colleagues the priests who are in Elephantine the fortress.

The welfare of our lord may the God of Heaven seek after abundantly at all times, and favor may He grant you before King Darius and the princes more than now a thousand times, and long life may He give you, and happy and strong may you be at all times.

Now, your servant Jedaniah and his colleagues thus say:

In the month of Tammuz, year 14 of Darius the king, when Arsames had departed and gone to the king, the priests of Khnub the god who are in Elephantine the fortress, in agreement with Vidranga who was Chief here, (said), saying,

"The Temple of YHW the God which is in Elephantine the fortress let them remove from there."

Afterwards, that Vidranga, the wicked, a letter did send to Naphaina his son, who was Troop Commander in Syene the fortress, saying,

"The Temple which is in Elephantine the fortress let them demolish."

Afterwards, Naphaina led the Egyptians with the other troops. They came to the fortress of Elephantine with their weapons, broke into that Temple, demolished it to the ground, and the stone pillars which were there—they smashed them. Moreover it happened (that the) 5 gateways of stone, built of hewn stone, which were in that Temple they demolished. And their doors, standing, and the bronze hinges of those doors, and the cedarwood roof—all of (these) which, with the rest of the fittings and other (things), which were there—all (of these) with fire they burned. But the basins of gold and silver and (other) things which were in that Temple—all (of these) they took and made their own.

And during the days of the king(s) of Egypt our fathers had built that Temple in Elephantine the fortress and when Cambyses entered Egypt—that Temple built he found it. And the temples of the gods of Egypt, all (of them), they overthrew, but anything in that Temple one did not damage.

And when this had been done (to us), we with our wives and our children sackcloth were wearing and fasting and praying to YHW the Lord of Heaven who let us gloat over that Vidranga, the cur. They removed the anklet from his feet and all goods which he had acquired were lost. And all persons who sought evil for that Temple, all (of them), were killed and we gazed upon them.

Moreover, before this—at the time that this evil was done to us—a letter we sent (to) our lord, and to Jehohanan the High Priest and his colleagues the priests who are in Jerusalem, and to Ostanes the brother of Anani and the nobles of the Jews. One (=a single) letter they did not send us.

Moreover, from the month of Tammuz, year 14 of King Darius and until this day, sackcloth we are wearing and are fasting; the wives of ours as widow(s) are made; (with) oil (we) do not anoint (ourselves) and wine do not drink.

Moreover, from that (time) and until (this) day, year 17 of Darius the king, meal-offering and ince[n]se and burnt-offering they did not make in that Temple.

Now, your servants Jedaniah and his colleagues and the Jews, all (of them) citizens of Elephantine, thus say:

If to our lord it is good, take thought of that Temple to (re)build (it) since they do not let us (re)build it. Regard your obligees and your friends who are here in Egypt. May a letter from you be sent to them about the Temple of YHW the God to (re)build it in Elephantine the fortress just as it had been built formerly.

And the meal-offering and the incense and the burnt-offering they will offer on the altar of YHW the God in your name and we shall pray for you at all times—we and our wives and our children and the Jews, all (of them) who are here. If they do thus until that Temple be (re)built, a merit you will have before YHW the God of Heaven more than a person who will offer him burnt-offering and sacrifices (whose) worth is as the worth of silver, 1 thousand talents and {about} gold.

About this we have sent (and) informed (you).

Moreover, all the(se) words in one (=a single) letter we sent in our name to Delaiah and Shelemiah sons of Sanballat governor of Samaria.

Moreover, about this which was done to us, all of it, Arsames did not know. On the 20th of Marcheshvan, year 17 of Darius the king.

Not unexpectedly, Hancock rejects the Ethiopian legend that Menelik, the son of the Queen of Sheba by Solomon, brought the Ark to Ethiopia. Hancock concludes that the Ark was removed by Temple priests during King Manasseh's reign (c. 687–642 B.C.E.), because Manasseh placed an idol and pagan altars in the Temple (2 Kings 21:2–7). In this, Hancock has the support of prominent Biblical scholar Menahem Haran, of the Hebrew University of Jerusalem. Unlike Hancock, however, Haran refuses to speculate as to what may have

A written reply to Jedaniah's letter has not been discovered; probably an oral response was brought back by the messenger who delivered the letter to Bagohi. This memorandum , written in the first person on a torn piece of papyrus and corrected by erasures and marginal additions, suggests that the Elephantine community did receive a response allowing them to rebuild the temple where meal- and incense-offerings could be offered:

Memorandum. What Bagohi and Delaiah said to me.

Memorandum. Saying, "You may say in Egypt before Arsames about the Altar-House of the God of Heaven which in Elephantine the fortress built was formerly before Cambyses (and) which Vidranga, that wicked (man) demolished in year 14 of King Darius: to (re)build it on its site as it was formerly and the meal-offering and the incense they shall offer upon that altar just as formerly was done."

In a draft letter to a high Persian official, Jedaniah and his colleagues clearly state that they will not make burnt-offerings at the temple if they are allowed to rebuild it:

Your servants—

Jedaniah son of Gema[riah] by name, 1; Mauzi son of Nathan by name, [1]; Shemaiah son of Haggai by name, 1; Hosea son of Jathom by name, 1; Hosea son of Nattun by name, 1: all (told) 5 persons, Syenians who are herdi[tary property-hold]ers in Elephantine the fortress— thus say:

If our lord [...] and our Temple of YHW the God be (re)built in Elephantine the fortress as it former[ly] was [bu]ilt—and sheep, ox, and goat as burnt-offering are [n]ot made there but (only) incense (and) meal-offering [they offer there]—and should our lord mak[e] a statement [about this, then] we shall give to the house of our lord si[lver ... and] a thousa[nd] ardabs of barley.

—Translations by Bezalel Porten.

happened to the Ark after it was removed from the Temple, although he does observe that during Manasseh's reign the entire country "was not a safe place for those who were loyal to the worship of Yahweh."[8]

According to one Ethiopian tradition, the Ark did not arrive in Ethiopia until after 470 B.C.E. This left Hancock with about a 200-year gap between its removal in Manasseh's reign and its arrival in Ethiopia—which he accounts for, at least in part, by the Ark's sojourn in Elephantine.

An Ethiopian Jewish priest now living in Jerusalem told Hancock about a tradition of his people that they had lived in Egypt before coming to Ethiopia. It was this that suggested to Hancock that the Ark had been taken first to the settlement of Jews in Egypt by the priests who would not allow it to be defiled by Manasseh's blasphemies. And the Jewish temple on Elephantine fit the bill!

Hancock's argument is not impossible. It is simply too speculative. He writes as a journalist, not as a historian. The remainder of this article will illustrate the difference between the two. I will not prove that it could not have happened, only that Hancock has not met the standards of professional historians in contending that it did happen, or even that it was likely to have happened.

Hancock notes quite correctly that the Elephantine temple, oriented towards Jerusalem, was apparently built in imitation of the Jerusalem Temple. Both had the same dimensions, and both had a cedarwood roof. From this Hancock concludes that it is "probable" that the Elephantine temple was built to house the Ark. "Probable" is much too strong a word here. "Possible" would be more accurate.

Another factor that intrigues Hancock is that animal sacrifice was practiced in the Elephantine temple. In about 620 B.C.E., King Josiah of Judah instituted a religious reform (it was Josiah who removed Manasseh's idol from the Jerusalem Temple and burned it in the Kidron Valley [2 Kings 23:6]). Josiah, as part of his religious reform, abolished animal sacrifice everywhere but in the Jerusalem Temple. Nevertheless, animal sacrifice continued at the Elephantine temple. Hancock concludes that the priests of the Elephantine temple considered the presence of the Ark adequate justification for the continuance of animal sacrifices, despite the ban that had issued from Jerusalem. But this is begging the question. There is no reason to assume any preexistent link between sacrifices and the presence of the Ark.

The more important point, however, is Hancock's contention that the Jews of Elephantine believed that "Yahweh resided physically in their temple."[9] For this, he relies on certain religious terminology in the papyri, and that's where he gets into trouble.

Hancock notes that "a number of papyri" speak "in no uncertain terms" of YHWH as dwelling in Elephantine.[10] Actually he

can refer only to a single papyrus, not a number of them. That papyrus, a contract for the sale of a house, does indeed refer to "YHW* the God who dwells in the fortress of Elephantine,"[11] and we shall treat that document below.

This single papyrus from Elephantine mentions "YHW the God dwelling in Yeb." *YHW* is a local variant of *YHWH*, the personal name of the Israelite God; *Yeb* is Egyptian for "Elephant Land."

The main source for our knowledge of the Elephantine temple is a draft letter[12] (or file copy), dated November 25, 407 B.C.E., written by Jedaniah son of Gemariah, leader of the Jewish community on Elephantine, and his priestly colleagues to one Bagohi, the governor of the Persian province of Yahud (Judah) in Jerusalem (see the sidebar, p. 129). While the name Bagohi is Persian (Persia ruled most of the Near East at that time), Bagohi may well have been Jewish, since the other governors of Judah during the fifth and fourth centuries B.C.E. all seem to have been Jews.[13] Jedaniah begins by flattering Bagohi with blessings and, at the end, appeals for help. The letter displays a keen awareness of Aramaic rhetorical style and is replete with the requisite epistolary formulae. The Jews of Elephantine have had a traumatic experience. Their temple has been destroyed.

The Jewish community at Elephantine was probably founded as a military installation in about 650 B.C.E. during Manasseh's reign. A fair implication from the historical documents,[14] including the Bible, is that Manasseh sent a contingent of Jewish soldiers to assist Pharaoh Psammetichus I (664–610 B.C.E.) in his Nubian campaign and to join Psammetichus in throwing off the yoke of Assyria, then the world superpower.

---

*The tetragrammaton *YHWH* (Yahweh), the name of the Israelite deity, never appears in texts from Elephantine. In the papyri, the regular form of the divine name is written *YHW*; in the ostraca, the divine name is *YHH*. It appears that this abbreviated version of the divine name was confined to vernacular usage, while sacred writings used the form *YHWH*.

Egypt gained independence, but Manasseh's revolt failed; the Jewish soldiers, however, remained in Egypt. Herodotus reports that in the reign of Psammetichus garrisons were posted at Elephantine, Daphnae and Marea.[15]

Perhaps as an accommodation to the Jews in Egypt who served as a buffer to renewed Assyrian control of Syro-Palestine (and also to consolidate their loyalty), Psammetichus permitted the Jews to build their temple. The Jews were not the only ones to benefit. The Aramean soldiers on the mainland at Aswan were also allowed to erect temples to their gods—Banit, Bethel, Nabu and the Queen of Heaven.[16] According to the above-cited letter of Jedaniah, the Elephantine temple was constructed sometime before the Persian conquest of Egypt in 525 B.C.E.: "During the days of the kings of Egypt [i.e., when Egypt was independent] our forefathers built that temple in the Elephantine fortress and when Cambyses [the Persian ruler who conquered Egypt in 525 B.C.E.] entered Egypt, he found that temple built."[17]

But the Jews needed more than permission from the Egyptian ruler to build a temple. According to Israelite tradition, foreign soil was impure soil. From Joshua to the prophets to the Babylonian exiles,[18] it was understood that cultic activities should not be performed outside the land of Israel. When the cured Aramean leper Naaman wanted to worship YHWH in his homeland, he took with him two mule-loads of Israelite earth (2 Kings 5:15ff).

So what would be the Jewish justification for erecting a sanctuary in Egypt? Hancock suggests the reason was that during the reign of Manasseh, priests from the Jerusalem Temple had brought the Ark with them.

Somewhat disingenuously, Hancock quotes me as follows in support of his view:

> Manasseh's reign was accompanied by much bloodshed (2 Kings 21:10–16) and it may be surmised that priests as well as prophets opposed his paganization. Some of these priests fled to Egypt, joined the Jewish garrison at Elephantine, and there ... erected the Temple to YHW.[19]

Hancock then notes that "Porten nevertheless remains puzzled by the fact that a Jewish temple could have been built at Elephantine at all."[20]

Hancock thus indicates that I had simply left open the question as to why the Jews of Elephantine felt free to build a temple.

Hancock is wrong, however. I did explain what I thought the likely justification was. And the reason had nothing to do with speculation that it was to house the Ark. My explanation was in the part of my text that Hancock omitted from the quotation and that he replaced with three dots to indicate the omission. Let me repeat the quotation, replacing the ellipsis with the complete text, putting the part that Hancock omitted in italics:

> Manasseh's reign was accompanied by much bloodshed (2 Kings 21:10–16) and it may be surmised that priests as well as prophets opposed his paganization. Some of these priests fled to Egypt, joined the Jewish garrison at Elephantine, and there *inspired by Isaiah's prophecy of a pillar to the Lord at the border of Egypt*, erected the Temple to YHW.

Isaiah uttered five eschatological oracles about what will be "on that day" when the "Lord will smite Egypt." The third oracle states, "On that day there will be an altar to the Lord in the midst of the land of Egypt and a pillar to the Lord at its border" (Isaiah 19:19). Elephantine is on Egypt's border. Isaiah's prophecy may well have inspired the Elephantine Jews during the oppressive years of Manasseh's reign. I conjectured that a sacred pillar to the Lord, in fulfillment of this prophecy, may have stood in the *adytum* (innermost sanctuary) of the Elephantine temple, just as a sacred pillar was placed in the *adytum* of the temple to Yahweh that archaeologists have excavated in Arad.[21]

In short, Hancock's placing the Ark in the Elephantine temple as a justification for its construction does not hold up. It is possible, but the evidence is very soft. I believe the justification was the passage from Isaiah predicting the erection of a pillar to the Lord at the border of Egypt.

From the letter to Bagohi as well as from other documents, we know what went on in the Elephantine temple before it was destroyed. Jedaniah writes that since the temple has been

136

destroyed, "meal offering, incense, and burnt offering [that is, animal sacrifice] were not offered in that temple."[22] The burnt offering (Hebrew *olah*) was one of the two major sacrifices practiced in Israel from earliest times.

We also have some idea of what the temple was like from the description of what was destroyed: The temple's stone pillars and five gateways were demolished; the cedarwood doors, roof and other fittings were burned (this is the source of our knowledge that the temple had a cedarwood roof); and gold, silver and other objects of value were looted.[23]

The temple was destroyed in 410 B.C.E. by Egyptian priests of the ram-god Khnum and their allies in connivance with the local Persian governor, an evil man named Vidranga. The reason for the destruction remains a question.[24] In Jedaniah's letter, he recalls that when the Persians conquered the country all the Egyptian temples were overthrown, but no damage was done to the Jewish temple. The implication is clear: Vidranga and the Egyptian priests had acted without authority in destroying this venerable Jewish religious establishment.[25] The Jews of Elephantine mourned the destruction of their temple; donned sackcloth; fasted; abstained from sexual intercourse, anointing and wine; and prayed for the downfall of those responsible. Finally, YHW, the Lord of Heaven, answered their prayers: Vidranga had been punished by his superiors and his property confiscated; it is even possible that he was executed.[26]

The Jews of Elephantine, the letter to Bagohi goes on to say, now need help (or permission) to rebuild their temple.

One may wonder whether the Egyptian priests of Khnum would not also have looted or destroyed the Ark if it had been in the Elephantine temple. Hancock does not stop to ask this question. Moreover, if the Ark had in fact been in Elephantine, would the Jews have needed permission of the Jerusalem authorities to rebuild the temple? And would the Jerusalem authorities have hesitated, as they did, in giving permission? Hancock does not address these questions either.

A Scholar at Work: Marriage Contract Mystery Ends Happily Ever After

By Bezalel Porten

I first examined the Aramaic papyri in the Brooklyn Museum in the fall of 1969. One of the documents that most fascinated me turned out to be the "Document of Wifehood" (perhaps more colloquially, the marriage contract) by which Anani, a Jewish temple official, took Tamet, an Egyptian slave, as his wife. She was given to him by her slave-master Meshullam, with whom Anani made the contract. As I was turning the document this way and that, from front (recto) to back (verso), conservator Kenneth Linsner, who was with me, pointed to some holes at the bottom of the back of the document.

"What's this writing?" he asked.

"What writing?" I looked more closely. There it was. On either side of one of the holes were a few Aramaic letters. "No one has ever noticed any writing there [at the bottom of the back of the document]." By "no one," I was of course referring to Emil G. Kraeling, because he was the only scholar who had seen these documents. It was he who had published them along with excellent photographs. But the published photograph of this document did not show the bottom of the back (verso), presumably to save space, but only the top of the back, where a single line of text appeared.

Unfortunately, most of the line of writing at the bottom of the back did not survive, as indicated by the good size hole in the middle of the line. I could see one word at the beginning (spr), which means "document" (in other contexts, "book") and the beginning of another word. On the other side of the hole were two other letters: mt. I immediately recognized these as the last two letters in Tamet's name. (Remember that Aramaic, like Hebrew, is written without vowels.) Here was the endorsement of the document—that is, the title that identified it when it was rolled and folded up.

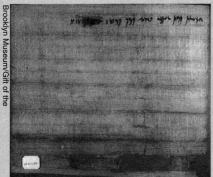

Important legal documents were stored by first rolling them up and pressing them flat. On the bottom of the back, which remained exposed by this rolling and flattening process, the scribe would write the "endorsement" that identified the document. The document was then reduced to a third of itself by folding in the two ends of the flattened document, still leaving part of the endorsement exposed. In this condition, the document was wrapped with string, and a daub of clay was placed over the knot to secure it. Into the soft clay, the seal of the owner or scribe was impressed.

Endorsements began with the word *spr*, "document," and followed a fixed formula, including a space after the word *spr* for a seal. The first letter of the second word in this endorsement was also preserved: It was the first letter of the word for wifehood. Then came the hole. After the hole were the last two letters in the name of Tamet. Based on these clues, as well as the size of the hole and the contents of the document on the other side, I was able to reconstruct the endorsement with considerable confidence: "Document of wifehood which Anani wrote for Tamet."

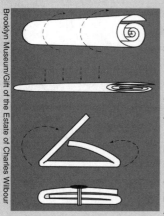

Kraeling knew as well as I did that documents like this have endorsements. But he published an entirely different endorsement to this document. According to Kraeling, the endorsement of this document read: "Tamet brought in to Anani in her hand silver, 1 karsh, 5 shekels."

Kraeling of course recognized that this language was not the usual form of an endorsement. He explained this allegedly stark deviation from the usual form of an endorsement in this way: "The 'endorsement' appearing on the outside of the roll is usually a memorandum enabling the owner of a number of sealed rolls to know what each is about. Sometimes, however, it has a supplementary recording function, as here."

The letter we have been discussing was not the first that the Jews of Elephantine had addressed to the Jerusalem authorities. It refers to at least one other such letter, and perhaps more, that, alas, had gone unanswered. The Jews of Elephantine now write also to the authorities in Samaria asking for help.

The earlier letters may have been sent by the regular postal service. Jedaniah's letter to Bagohi, however, was delivered to Jerusalem by personal messenger, perhaps by Jedaniah himself.

This is an entirely *ad hoc* explanation. No other example of such a "supplementary recording" has ever been found.

What Kraeling thought was the endorsement was the single line at the top of the back of the document. Kraeling was a marvelous editor of the papyri, and we may easily forgive him for this lapse. None of the other documents in the archive had any text on the back of the document, except the endorsement. So when Kraeling saw the single line of text at the top of the back of the document, he assumed it was the endorsement. What he failed to notice—or perhaps, to be more accurate, failed to appreciate—was that the

endorsements on the other documents were always at the bottom of the back of the document, never at the top. Had he appreciated this fact, he would surely have looked at the bottom of the back and noticed the letters that Linsner called to my attention as I turned the document over.

What, then, was the line at the top of the back? It was simply the end of the text that ran over onto the back. It is clear from the erasures and changes in the main text, as well as the different inks used (determined by microscopic examination and confirmed by infrared photographs) that this document was heavily negotiated. Among the issues was the amount of Tamet's dowry. Obviously, there had been very considerable haggling over it, meagre though it was. Finally, at the end of the negotiation, Meshullam apparently gave in and agreed to pay Anani an additional karsh and five shekels—in cash! This is attested by the runover line at the top of the back of the document, an addition to Tamet's dowry that came in the process of the haggling that continued down through the final stages of the redaction of the document.

Unfortunately, no one could catch Kraeling's error from the publication since the published photographs show only the alleged endorsement and not the rest of the verso (back), which was supposedly blank.

Jedaniah promises that if the Jerusalem authorities give permission to rebuild the temple at Elephantine, the Elephantine Jews will pray for Bagohi "at all times."[27] If Bagohi helps to achieve the rebuilding of the Elephantine temple, he "shall have a merit (*tsedakah*) before YHW the God of Heaven more than a person who offers to him burnt offering and sacrifices worth a thousand talents of silver."[28]

Whether the Jewish community of Elephantine received a written reply to this letter is not known. Probably the response was oral, perhaps brought back by the messenger who delivered the letter to Jerusalem. Some response is reflected in a difficult first-person memorandum by Bagohi of Jerusalem and Delaiah of Samaria, written on an already torn piece of papyrus, and corrected by erasures and marginal and supralinear additions (see the sidebar, p. 129).[29]

The Jerusalem authorities had doubtless faced a dilemma. A negative answer would have given comfort and support to the Elephantine Jews' enemies. A positive answer would have compromised Jerusalem's cultic centrality. The Jerusalem authorities apparently opted for a compromise: Permission to rebuild was given, but no longer were burnt offerings (animal sacrifices) to be offered. According to the memorandum, the Jews were to speak before the Egyptian authorities about the "Altar-house of the God of Heaven which was built in Elephantine the fortress ... to rebuild it on its site as it was formerly and the meal-offering and the incense they may offer on that altar just as formerly was done."[30] Thus, the offerings were limited to cereals and incense. (Interestingly, the prophet Malachi, speaking in the name of the Lord, rejects a blemished offering at the restored Jerusalem Temple [Malachi 1:8], and notes that incense and meal offerings are made to the Lord "from one end of the earth to the other" [Malachi 1:11]. If from "one end of the earth to the other," certainly such offerings are kosher at Elephantine.) Even though Josiah's reform had centralized all cultic worship in Jerusalem, this compromise suggested that the Jerusalem governor was willing to concede that the Elephantine temple, which preceded that reform and existed outside the land of Israel, was legitimate—but in a limited way. Blood on the altar was to be allowed only in Jerusalem.

Yet if the Ark were in Elephantine, wouldn't the Jerusalem authorities have allowed burnt offerings? Again, this is a question Hancock does not ask. Indeed, Hancock contends that the presence of the Ark at Elephantine provided the original authorization to offer animal sacrifices. If true, the Jerusalem authorities' refusal to allow animal sacrifice in the rebuilt temple certainly militates against Hancock's contention that the Ark was there.

That animal sacrifice was forbidden is reflected in still another document in the archive, a draft of a letter (or file copy) to a high Persian official seeking authorization to rebuild the temple (see the sidebar, p. 129).[31] If such authorization is granted, the temple would be rebuilt as before, except, however, that "sheep, ox, and goat shall not be made there as burnt-offering but (only) incense and meal-offering." The Jews also agreed to pay for the Persian permission: "an amount of silver [the amount did not survive] and a thousand *ardabs* of barley." (That's a lot of barley, enough to feed about 540 men for a month.)

Not until 1953 did we learn of the probability that the Elephantine temple was rebuilt. That was when the documents recovered by Wilbour in 1893 were published following the death of his daughter and the opening of the trunk in the New York

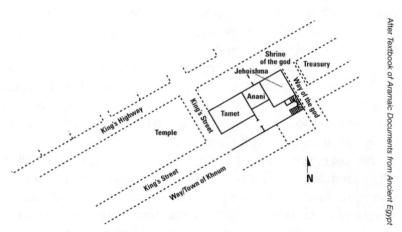

After Textbook of Aramaic Documents from Ancient Egypt

Documents from Anani's private archive allow us to reconstruct the layout of the Jewish district from just before the Elephantine temple's destruction in 410 B.C.E. to its reconstruction several years later.

In 437 B.C.E., Anani acquired abandoned property that, over the next 35 years, he parceled out to his wife Tamet, his daughter Jehoishma and his son-in-law Ananiah. His estate was strategically located between the Persian royal treasury to the east and the Jewish temple to the west. In 404 B.C.E., Anani mentions a new "house of the shrine of the god," probably associated with the cult of Khnum, and a protecting wall called "the way of the god." Built by the Egyptians, the wall ran between Anani's house and the royal treasury. In 402 B.C.E., according to the archive, the Temple of YHW still stood to the west of Anani's property.

warehouse. Wilbour's hoard contained a private archive of a minor temple official named Ananiah son of Azariah. He was nicknamed Anani and that is what we shall call him; it is difficult not to be on familiar terms with him after reading his archive.[32]

In one of the documents in this archive (a "document of wife-hood"), Anani identifies his wife Tamet as an Egyptian slave belonging to Meshullam son of Zaccur. Tamet brings a miniscule dowry to the marriage, but the document reveals haggling over even this (see the sidebar, p. 137). The document of wifehood is dated August 9, 449 B.C.E.

Twelve years later, on September 13, 437 B.C.E., Anani takes title to a house. It is a piece of abandoned property acquired from a Caspian couple, but Anani nonetheless treats it as an estate that he parcels out in stages over the course of the next 35 years, first to his wife Tamet, then to his daughter and finally to his son-in-law. And although it was not much as property goes, it was strategically located—with the Persian royal treasury on the east and the Jewish temple on the west.

Three years later, after fixing up the house (and perhaps after the birth of their daughter), Anani bestows upon Tamet a room in the house. According to this document, there is no change in the neighbors to the house. Both the royal Persian treasury and the Jewish temple are still there.

Almost seven years later, on June 12, 427 B.C.E., Meshullam (the slavemaster of Tamet) in his old age makes a testamentary change (to take effect at his death) in the status of Tamet and her daughter. Tamet is freed and their daughter, formerly the daughter of a slave-wife, becomes Meshullam's adopted daughter: "I released you as a free (person) at my death ... you are released from the shade to the sun ... you are released to God." To which mother and daughter respond, "We shall serve you as a son or daughter supports his father, in your lifetime."

Still seven years more and the daughter marries; on July 11, 420 B.C.E., Anani gives the daughter (and presumably her husband) the use of a room in the house. In addition, this daughter of a slave even receives a generous dowry of 78 shekels from her adoptive brother Zaccur (the son of her slavemaster Meshullam).

Then for 16 years the archive is silent. In 410 B.C.E., the

Elephantine temple was destroyed, as we have seen. On November 25, 404 B.C.E., Anani makes a bequest in contemplation of death in which he assures his daughter that, although she is not to receive immediate title to the property, Anani is indeed "giving" it to her to take effect, however, only upon his death. By this time, there have been some changes in the neighbors. One neighbor's house is no longer there, but adjoining it is "the house of the shrine of the god." On another side is "the protecting wall that the Egyptians built; that is, the way of the god" where the royal Persian treasury had been.

On March 9, 402 B.C.E., again after the destruction of the Elephantine temple in 410 B.C.E., Anani gives his daughter immediate full rights to the room to which he had previously given her only the right of use. From the delineation of the boundaries of the house, we now learn that the "protecting wall which the Egyptians built" has not replaced the treasury but adjoins it "wall to wall."

What appears to have happened is that sometime after Anani's first bequest in 420 B.C.E., when the royal treasury still bordered his house,[33] the Egyptians cut a swath away from the treasury and built a protecting wall on either side of this "divine way" that led to the newly erected "house of the shrine of the god," doubtless associated with the Egyptian cult of Khnum. Whenever that event occurred, it was memorable enough to warrant specific mention in a legal contract.

Finally, on December 13, 402 B.C.E., Anani and his wife Tamet sell the house to their son-in-law. The Temple of YHW still lies to the west.[34] By this time Anani and his wife have been married for 47 years. In this document, she is no longer "Tamet, the handmaiden" of Meshullam (her slavemaster), but Meshullam's "main beloved" and "the one who belongs to his inner chamber." She is then given a glorious history to enhance her present status. More importantly for our purposes, in the opening lines, she is designated "servitor of YHW the God dwelling (in) Elephantine the fortress."[35]

In previous documents, Anani had been designated "servitor of YHW in Elephantine." In this final document, the scribe applies the title to Tamet and inserts the word "dwelling": Instead of referring to YHW in Elephantine, we now have

YWH dwelling in Elephantine. Is this an indication that by this time, in 402 B.C.E., the Jews had rebuilt their House of YHW that lay across the street? From this document, it would appear so.

Hancock heavily relies on the fact that, as he says, "a number of papyri speak of [YHW]—in no uncertain terms—as 'dwelling' there."[36] In fact, the papyri speak of this only once; there are not "a number of papyri." And this single document is dated after the destruction of the Elephantine temple in 410 B.C.E. If it proves anything, it is that YHW continued to dwell at Elephantine when the Elephantine temple had probably been rebuilt. If the "dwelling" of YHW was the Ark, as Graham Hancock claims, it survived the destruction of 410 B.C.E.

But, more fundamentally, it does not follow that if God is said to dwell in Elephantine, his Ark is there. Hancock argues that "the Elephantine Jews frequently spoke of the deity dwelling in their temple as 'the Lord of Hosts.'" Since this term "was frequently used in connection with the Ark," Hancock concludes that the Ark must have been in Elephantine.[37]

First, the phrase "the Lord of Hosts" is used not "frequently," but only two or three times. And the word dwelling, as we have seen, is used only once—and then after the Elephantine temple had been destroyed. The term "Lord of Hosts" occurs approximately 75 times in the contemporaneous books of Haggai, Zechariah 1–8 and Malachi without reference to the Ark. The use of the epithet "Lord of Hosts" is no indication of the location of the Ark. In Ezra 7:15, YHWH (the Israelite God) is said to "dwell" in Jerusalem even after the Temple has been destroyed and the Ark has disappeared.

To summarize, Manasseh's revolt against his Assyrian overlords may have led him to an alliance with Egypt. In that connection, he most likely dispatched a contingent of Jewish soldiers to Egypt. At the same time, his profanation of the Jerusalem Temple and his harsh repressive policies may well have resulted in the flight into Egypt of disaffected Jerusalem priests. Both the soldiers and the priests eventually found their way up the Nile to Elephantine. There, under Egyptian tutelage, they built a temple to YHW.

The notion that these fugitive priests spirited the Ark away from Jerusalem to rescue it from the clutches of Manasseh is nothing but bald speculation; it is not historical reconstruction. None of the evidence cited to support this unscholarly speculation holds up under careful scrutiny.

The phrase "the dwelling of YHW(H)," which appears in a single document from Elephantine, does not indicate that the Ark dwelt there. As we know from Ezra, YHWH dwelt in Jerusalem even after the Temple was destroyed by the Babylonians, rebuilt by Zerubbabel and dedicated on March 12, 515 B.C.E. (Ezra 6:15). He dwelt all over.

Similarly with the incense offerings and burnt offerings at Elephantine: They were offered all over, as Malachi implies, not just where the Ark was located.

Nor is there any connection between the epithet "Lord of Hosts" (which is used in reference to YHW at Elephantine and countless times in the Bible in reference to YHWH), on the one hand, and the location of the Ark of the Covenant, on the other.

The fact that a Jewish temple was built at Elephantine may be explained by Isaiah 19:19: "In that day, there shall be an altar to the Lord inside the land of Egypt and a pillar to the Lord at its border." The Elephantine temple may have been authorized pursuant to this prophecy, but there is absolutely nothing in the Bible or anywhere else to suggest that it was built to house the Ark of the Covenant.

---

1. Graham Hancock, *The Sign and the Seal: The Quest for the Lost Ark of the Covenant* (New York: Crown, 1992), pp. 438–442.

2. For *Biblical Archaeology Review*'s review, see the previous chapter in this book.

3. John A. Wilson, *Signs and Wonders upon Pharaoh* (Chicago, 1964), p. 101. His book is the source for the information on Wilbour.

4. In the papyri, the island is called *Yb* ("Elephant Land"). The name Elephantine may derive from the fact that ivory was transshipped there from Nubia.

5. Emil G. Kraeling, *The Brooklyn Museum Aramaic Papyri* (New Haven: Yale Univ. Press, 1953), p. 10.

6. Kraeling, "New Light on the Elephantine Colony," *Biblical Archaeologist* 15 (1952), p. 53, fig. 3; Abraham Joseph Sachs, "The Answer to a Puzzle," *Biblical Archaeologist* 15 (1952), p. 89.

7. Eduard Sachau, *Aramäische Papyrus und Ostraka aus einer jüdischen Militärkolonie zu Elephantine* (Leipzig, 1911).

8. Menahem Haran, *apud* Hancock, *Sign and Seal*, p. 423.

9. Hancock, *Sign and Seal*, p. 439.

10. Hancock, *Sign and Seal*, pp. 439–440.

11. See Bezalel Porten and Ada Yardeni, *Textbook of Aramaic Documents from Ancient Egypt Newly Copied, Edited and Translated into Hebrew and English* (Jerusalem: Academon, 1986–1993; Winona Lake, IN: Eisenbrauns [distributor]), vol. 2, B3.13:2. All quotations of Elephantine texts are taken from this series known as *TAD*: *TAD* A=vol. 1; *TAD* B=vol. 2; *TAD* C=vol. 3.

12. *TAD* A4.7. The letter, although well preserved, contains many erasures, corrections, words inserted above the line, and so on. The writing appears to have been transcribed hastily compared to other documents in the collection. Another fragmentary copy of this letter was also found (*TAD* A4.8). The date of the letter is determined by using the conversion table in R.A. Parker and W.H. Dubberstein's *Babylonian Chronology 626 B.C.-A.D. 75* (Providence, 1956).

13. Porten, *Archives from Elephantine* (Berkeley, CA: Univ. of California, 1968; revised edition, Leiden: Brill, forthcoming), p. 290.

14. Especially the letter of Aristeas. See Leonard J. Greenspoon, "Mission to Alexandria," *Bible Review 5:4*, August 1989.

15. Herodotus, *History* II.30.

16. *TAD* A2.1:1, 2.2:1, 2.3:1, 2.4:1.

17. *TAD* A4.7:13–14.

18. Joshua 22; Hosea 9:3ff; Amos 7:17; Jeremiah 16:13; Ezekiel 4:13; Psalm 137.

19. Porten, *Archives*, pp. 119–120.

20. Hancock, *Sign and Seal*, p. 441.

21. See Ze'ev Herzog, Miriam Aharoni and Anson Rainey, "Arad—An Ancient Israelite Fortress with a Temple to Yahweh," *Biblical Archaeology Review* 13:2 (March/April 1987).

22. *TAD* A4.7:21–22.

23. *TAD* A4.7:9–13.

24. See my discussion in *Archives from Elephantine* (Berkeley, CA: Univ. of California, 1968), pp. 284–289.

25. *TAD* A4.7:6–9; 13–14.

26. *Archives*, pp. 287–288; *TAD* A4.7:15–17.

27. *Archives*, p. 114; *TAD* A4.7:23–26.

28. *Archives*, p. 115; *TAD* A4.7:27–28.

29. *TAD* A4.9.

30. *TAD* A4.9.

31. *TAD* A4.10.

32. This archive was newly collated and restored by the paleographer Dr. Ada Yardeni and myself in 1987 and published in 1989 with English and Hebrew translations and full-size hand copy (*TAD* B3.1–13).

33. *TAD* B3.7:6–7.

34. *TAD* B3.12:18–19.

35. *TAD* B3.12:3, 11, 24.

36. Hancock, *Sign and Seal*, pp. 439–440.

37. Hancock, *Sign and Seal*, p. 440.

"In the time of King Herod, after Jesus was born in Bethlehem of Judea, wise men from the East came to Jerusalem, asking, 'Where is the child who has been born king of the Jews? For we have observed his star at its rising, and have come to pay him homage.'"

(Matthew 2:1-2)

Part VI

THE STAR OF BETHLEHEM

The wondrous star that hovered over Bethlehem at Jesus' birth has long mystified Bible scholars and astronomers alike. Attempts to identify the star with specific celestial phenomena have been inconclusive at best, leading many to dismiss the gospel account as a beautiful but imaginative myth.

As Assyriologist Simo Parpola notes in the following chapter, the wise men from the East were, in fact, astronomers—that's what the title magus *means. And in Eastern astronomy, certain celestial phenomena were interpreted as portents of the birth of kings. According to Parpola, a rare celestial occurrence in the late first millennium B.C. may well have been understood by the Babylonians as a sign that a new, divinely appointed king had been born.*

CHAPTER 11

What the Wise Men Knew

Babylonian Astronomy Dates Jesus' Birth

Simo Parpola

———•◦•———

According to the Gospel of Matthew, after Jesus was born "magi from the East arrived in Jerusalem, asking, 'Where is the child who has been born king of the Jews? We have observed the rising of his star, and we have come to pay him homage'" (Matthew 2:2). I believe that Babylonian astronomy may provide the key to identifying the star and to dating Jesus' birth: That's because the Gospel of Matthew tells us that the magi—astronomers from the East—believed that the star would lead them to a new king. Why? What did the magi know?

Herod clearly felt that the magi knew something. He was deeply disturbed by their news. He called his chief priests and scribes before him and asked them where such a child would be born. They said Bethlehem (where King David, whose scion would be the messiah, had been born). Herod then instructed the magi to continue on their journey to Bethlehem: "Go and search diligently for the child," Herod advised. "When you have found him, bring me word so that I may also go and pay him homage" (Matthew 2:8). Once they found the child, Herod advised, they should report back to him. Secretly, the king planned to destroy the infant.

The magi set out on the road to Bethlehem. "The star that they had seen in its rising went ahead of them until it stopped above the place where the child lay. At the sight of the star, they were overjoyed. Entering the house, they saw the child with Mary his mother, and bowed to the ground in homage to him; then they opened their treasures and offered him gifts: gold, frankincense and myrrh" (Matthew 2:9–11). Having been warned in a dream of Herod's malicious intent, the magi returned home "by another road" (Matthew 2:12).

The term Matthew uses, *magoi* ("magi" in English), refers to Persian astronomers or scholars, although it is often translated simply as "wise men." Matthew does not mention the names or the number of these wise men, but according to later Christian tradition, there were three: Balthassar, Melchior and Caspar. Balthassar is a Greek corruption of the Babylonian name Belshazzar (*Bel-shar-usur*) familiar from the Book of Daniel; it means "O Lord, protect the king." Melchior, which means "The king is my light," is an Aramaic name often encountered in Assyrian and Babylonian texts. Caspar (sometimes spelled Gaspar) is a Roman corruption of Gondophares (Gadaspar), a Parthian name (the language of the people who ruled Persia in Matthew's time). The names of the magi suggest that they came from Babylon, a Parthian royal city and one of the most important centers of astronomical and astrological knowledge of the day.

From its beginnings in the early second millennium B.C.E., Babylonian astronomy was linked with astrology and divination. The royal courts used astronomy to interpret celestial events, which were understood as portents sent from the gods to the king. Every day, month, part of the sky and celestial body or phenomenon had a significance of its own. An eclipse of the moon, for example, might be interpreted as a sign that the king would die. By the fifth century B.C.E., personal horoscopes were being used to predict an individual's future based on the positions of the planets in various constellations at the time of his or her birth (that is, based on the astrological significance of both the planets in the night sky at the time of the birth and the constellations in front of which the planets appeared).

The work of Babylonian astronomers was, of course, limited to what could be seen by the naked eye, for the telescope would not be invented until the Renaissance. In planetary terms, this meant astronomers could observe the movements of Mercury, Venus, Mars, Saturn and Jupiter, but not Uranus, Neptune and Pluto. Nevertheless, between 220 B.C.E. and 75 C.E., Babylonian astronomy had advanced so far that all significant phenomena involving these five visible planets and the moon could be accurately computed in advance. This is demonstrated in the many Babylonian astronomical almanacs that have survived from this period. Like modern almanacs, the Babylonian texts were prepared a year in advance and provide a month-by-month account of what would be seen in the night sky. The data include lunar and solar eclipses, solstices and equinoxes, the first and last dates when stars would be visible in the night sky, planetary positions in relation to the zodiacal signs, conjunctions (when celestial bodies appear closest to each other in the sky) and oppositions (when a planet appears on the opposite side of the Earth from the sun; this usually occurs when the planet is closest to Earth, as in the diagram on p. 157).

Today, we know of several astronomical events that enlivened the night sky in the last years of the first millennium B.C.E. and the beginning of the first millennium C.E. Identifying one of these as the Star of Bethlehem would give us the date of Jesus' birth. For although today we celebrate the birth of Jesus in 1 C.E., most scholars believe he was actually born sometime between 7 and 4 B.C.E., based on the Gospel of Matthew, which indicates that Jesus was born late in the reign of King Herod of Judea, who died in 4 B.C.E.[1]

Among the possible candidates is an exceptional light phenomenon—possibly a nova (a star that suddenly increases in brightness) or a supernova (a giant stellar explosion)—known from ancient Chinese records to have occurred in the constellation of Capricorn in 5 B.C.E. However, unlike the Star of Bethlehem in the Gospel of Matthew, novas do not move but remain stationary in relation to the fixed stars, so this possibility must be rejected as unsatisfactory. Chinese and Roman sources also record an appearance of Halley's comet from August to

October in 12 B.C.E.; but this date is too far from the death of Herod to be considered seriously. No other suitable observations of comets are known from this period.

Another possibility is a conjunction of Venus and Jupiter in 2 B.C.E. During a conjunction, two planets appear close to each other in the night sky. In 2 B.C.E., Jupiter and Venus came so close together that they appeared to merge into a single brilliant star, although only for a very short duration—a maximum of two hours before their setting. Nevertheless, this conjunction must be dismissed because it occurred after Herod's death.

The only remaining candidate is a conjunction of Jupiter and Saturn in 7 B.C.E.[2] Already in 1604 Johannes Kepler associated this event with the birth of Jesus. However, Jupiter and Saturn did not come close enough to each other during this conjunction to be seen as a single exceptionally bright star. Rather, they remained at least one degree apart (about two diameters of the moon), leading one scholar to conclude: "This fact renders it impossible to explain the Star of Bethlehem with reference to that particular conjunction."[3]

It thus seems that from the viewpoint of modern science, the Star of Bethlehem cannot be satisfactorily explained. We will have better luck, however, if we turn to ancient science, which sheds light on how the magi themselves would have understood these celestial phenomena, in particular the conjunction of 7 B.C.E. For although modern scholars might find it "impossible" to identify this conjunction of Saturn and Jupiter with the magi's star, Babylonian astronomers used the term kakkabu, "star," to refer to a single star or planet as well as a constellation.

Further evidence of how ancient astronomers would have understood this conjunction has been revealed by excavations in Babylon, which have uncovered four clay tablets bearing astronomical computations for the year 7 B.C.E.[4] This almanac indicates that, from the beginning of the year, Jupiter and Saturn were continuously visible in Pisces for 11 months. In other words, for most of the year the constellation Pisces served as a backdrop for the planets Jupiter and Saturn as they traveled slowly through the night sky. The movements, stationary points, and risings and settings of both planets are accurately registered month by month.

They came closest together on three nights in May, October and December. It appears from the almanac that toward the end of the conjunction, Mars also moved into Pisces; it was visible near Jupiter and Saturn in mid-February.

That the almanac survives in four copies is remarkable, and, indeed, quite exceptional. The overwhelming majority (85 percent) of the known almanacs are available in one copy only, and only two other almanacs are available in four or more copies. Unlike modern almanacs, Babylonian almanacs were not drawn up for the general public but for the private use of a handful of experts, and they were guarded as great scholarly secrets. That so many copies exist of this one is all the more surprising when one considers its date: Cuneiform texts become rare in the latter half of the first century B.C.E. (the latest known cuneiform tablet dates from 75 C.E. and there are only four cuneiform tablets altogether from the Christian Era).

The great number of copies has an obvious explanation, however: An 11-month conjunction of Jupiter and Saturn in Pisces is an extremely rare event, occurring only once every 800 years. Because of the slow rotational velocity of both Jupiter (which has a 12-year orbit around the sun) and Saturn (29.5 years), any conjunction of these planets (the so-called "great conjunction") will only happen every 20 years. The 11-month conjunction of 7 B.C.E., however, was special in that the planets met three times in succession in the same constellation. It can occur only when both planets are in opposition to the sun; that is, the sun is on the opposite side of the Earth from the planets. Since 7 B.C.E. a triple conjunction of Saturn and Jupiter has been observed only twice, in the years 786 and 1583.

For the ancient Babylonian magi, however, the conjunction was not only important astronomically, but astrologically and politically.

In the Babylonian system, Jupiter, the largest and brightest planet, was known as the star of Marduk, the supreme god of Babylon. Saturn, the second largest planet, was the star of the king, the earthly representative of the god. The Babylonians called Saturn *Kaiwānu*, "The Steady One." The constellation Pisces was associated with Ea, the god of wisdom, life and creation. Pisces was also the last sign in the zodiac—that is, the last constellation that the sun passed through each year. The conjunction of the planets in Pisces accordingly portended two things: the end of the old world order and the birth of a new savior king chosen by God. No Babylonian interpretation of this particular conjunction is extant—surely because of the great rarity of the event—but we know that interpretations of planetary conjunctions were based on an analysis of the astrological significance of the planets and the accompanying circumstances, particularly the zodiacal sign in which the conjunction took place. The fact that Mars, the star of Nergal, the god of war,[5] joined the conjunction in its final phase signified that the new king was to come from the West, specifically, from Syria-Palestine, for Mars was the star of Amurru or the West (Syria-Palestine) in the Babylonian system.

The prediction of such a king would have held wide interest in 7 B.C.E., when a power vacuum of sorts prevailed in the Near East. The Seleucid Empire created by the successors of Alexander the Great had collapsed in 64 B.C.E., and its remnants, which included Judea, had been annexed to Rome as a province named Syria. The power of Rome had not yet been consolidated in the area, however. Even after Augustus changed Rome into an autocratic monarchy in 27 B.C.E., his authority was questioned in the East, for the Roman emperor, unlike the Seleucid kings and their predecessors, did not derive his authority from God. For this reason, many people considered Roman rule illegitimate and hoped that a local Near Eastern king appointed by God would drive the Romans out of the country and create a better world. These messianic expectations are recorded by Josephus and reflected in the Dead Sea Scrolls.

The conjunction of 7 B.C.E. would have been interpreted as a portent of the birth of precisely this kind of king. The political vistas opened by it would not have escaped the attention of any Babylonian astrologer.

When the year 7 B.C.E. began, Jupiter was already visible in the night sky. Saturn appeared soon after, on the third day of the first month, Nisan (at the beginning of April). The planets met for the first time on May 27, rising in the east at about 2:00 a.m., the brighter Jupiter first, and Saturn, considerably dimmer, soon after it.

The Night Sky in 7 B.C.E.

The apparent motion of the planets against the night sky is erratic. The outer planets Mars, Jupiter and Saturn, for example, spend most of the year traveling eastward against the backdrop of stars, but every so often, and almost always at separate times, each planet will appear to make a loop or switchback in its journey. It will slow down, "stop" and then travel back toward the west for a short distance—in what astronomers call *retrograde motion*—then it will slow down again, stop and resume travel in an easterly direction.

In the 16th century, the Polish astronomer Copernicus realized that the retrograde motion of planets was actually an illusion. The apparent back-

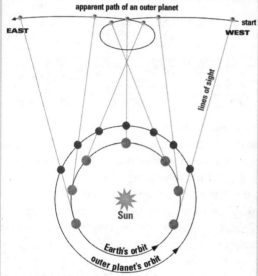

ward motion of the planets that are farther from the sun than the Earth—Mars, Jupiter and Saturn—against the backdrop of stars occurs each time the Earth overtakes or "laps" these slower planets as we make our yearly journey around the sun. The Earth overtakes an outer planet when it is in opposition to the sun; that is, the sun, Earth and planet are aligned with the Earth in the middle, as shown here.

In this drawing, Earth and an outer planet are shown at various stages in their orbits around the sun. The looping line at top shows how the outer planet appears to travel across the sky, starting in the west (at right), when viewed from Earth. As Earth overtakes the planet, the planet appears to loop backward, although of course it's still moving forward.

What makes the events of 7 B.C.E. so unusual, astronomically speaking, is that the Earth overtook both Jupiter and Saturn at the same time, when they were in conjunction. It's very rare for these two planets to come into conjunction at all—it only happens once every 20 years—and it's even less common for this to happen when they are in opposition and the Earth is passing them, making them both go into apparent retrograde motion at about the same time.

This meant that in 7 B.C.E. the two slowest planets lingered for a long time—11 months—together in the same small corner of the sky (in Pisces).

While in Pisces, they came into conjunction—passed especially close to each other in the sky—three different times.

This diagram depicts the similar, looping paths these planets took that year starting in the west (at right) and moving, at first, in an easterly direction (to the left). The Babylonian year began in the month of Nisan (our April). Saturn first appeared on about the third of Nisan (April 4 in the drawing) and moved slowly eastward from night to night. Jupiter appeared a few weeks later, on April 24. Jupiter was moving more quickly in its smaller orbit and caught up to Saturn on May 27—the date of the first conjunction.

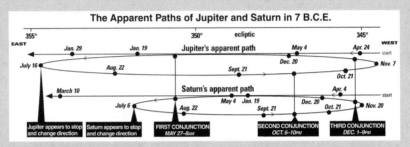

The Apparent Paths of Jupiter and Saturn in 7 B.C.E.

For the next couple months, both planets appeared to travel in the typical easterly direction, but Earth was gaining fast. As the Earth began to overtake Saturn, Saturn appeared to slow its eastward advance, stop and then switch direction on July 6. Jupiter did the same thing when Earth passed by it: On July 16 it appeared to stop and change direction. Now both planets appeared to move from east to west across the sky, with Saturn in the lead once again. On October 6, 7 B.C.E., at 10 p.m., Jupiter caught up with Saturn. This was the second conjunction of the year, made even more striking by the full moon that shone nearby that evening.

The planets continued to travel west until November. As Earth moved farther ahead, the planets appeared to pause for a second time: Jupiter on November 7, Saturn on November 20. They then appeared once again to travel in their usual, easterly direction. Saturn again was in the lead, but Jupiter quickly caught up. On December 1, at 9 p.m., the two planets came into conjunction for the third and final time that year. It would be another 20 years before they would meet again, another 200 years before they met in Pisces and another 800 years before they would meet in a triple conjunction.

The second meeting of the planets occurred on the 22nd of Tishri (October 6). Just as Mars was the star of Amurru (the West), Tishri was known as the month of Amurru. This second meeting may have inspired the magi to head West. That they chose to visit Herod's court is natural, as he was unquestionably one of the most powerful kings of Syria-Palestine.

The magi would have seen a brilliant and suggestive sight. Jupiter and Saturn were in opposition to the sun and shining at their brightest, with Jupiter (the star of the supreme god) appearing twice as bright as Sirius, the brightest star. Appearing directly above Saturn (the star of the king), Jupiter thus seemed to embrace and protect Saturn in its light. The conjunction was visible through the whole night, setting in the West. For the magi, the significance resided in the astrological message, not the appearance: Matthew nowhere stresses the brightness of the star.

The journey of about 750 miles from Babylon to Jerusalem took about three weeks by donkey or camel. If the magi left for Syria-Palestine in early Tishri (October), they would have arrived there well before November 7, when Jupiter reached a stationary point (its second) and for a moment seemed to come to a stop. This occurs whenever the Earth, traveling at a faster rate in its smaller, inner orbit, catches up with Jupiter (or any outer planet). As the Earth overtakes the planet, Jupiter appears from our vantage point to pause in the sky, then to travel backward (westward) in retrograde motion until Earth has passed by. The planet then pauses a second time and turns back in an easterly direction (see drawing, p. 158). On November 20, Saturn reached its (second) stationary point. Both dates—the 7th for Jupiter and 20th for Saturn—would fit Matthew's description of a star stopping above Bethlehem.

The third conjunction occurred at the time of the full moon, on the 14th of Kislev (December 1), about three weeks before the winter solstice, when the Babylonians held their annual celebration of the victory of their savior god, Nabû, over the forces of darkness. The magi may well have associated the birth of the child they were looking for with this festival, for the Mesopotamian king was commonly regarded as an incarnation of Nabû. Interestingly, the Babylonians proclaimed Nabû's victory as "good tidings" (*bussurāti*) to all the people. *Bussurtu,* "good tidings," is the same word as Hebrew/Aramaic *besorah,* of which the Biblical *euangelion* (gospel) is a Greek translation.

In Luke, the angel uses this very term to announce Jesus' birth to the shepherds keeping watch over their flock by night: "Do not be afraid; for see—I am bringing you good news [*euangelion = bussurtu*] of great joy for all the people: to you is born this day in the city of David a Savior, who is the Messiah, the Lord" (Luke 2:10–11).

How could a star lead the magi to Jerusalem and Bethlehem? These Babylonian astronomers would have "followed" a star only based on its astrological significance. In 7 B.C.E., they read the message of the "star"—that a messiah-king would be born in Syria-Palestine—and they headed to a leading political center in the region, King Herod's court. There they were directed to Bethlehem; as they traveled, both the planet of the king (Saturn) and the planet of the supreme god (Jupiter) would have paused in the sky, as planets do when the Earth overtakes them in their orbit. In late December, at the winter solstice, the magi would have rejoiced with good news, or *bussurāti*: Their savior king was born—several years before the Christian Era even began!

---

1. The situation is complicated by the Gospel of Luke, however, which indicates that Jesus was born during a worldwide census conducted by the Syrian governor; from extrabiblical sources, we know of a census conducted in 6 C.E. (although not of the scope described by Luke). Most scholars find the worldwide census described in Luke too improbable to be historical and thus favor the account in Matthew.

2. The American astronomer Michael Molnar (*The Star of Bethlehem: The Legacy of the Magi* [New Brunswick, NJ: Rutgers Univ. Press, 1999]) recently presented a theory that the star of Bethlehem should be identified with two occultations of Jupiter by the moon in Aries in 6 B.C.E. This theory must be rejected, however, since in Babylonian astrology the occultation of Jupiter by the moon signified the death of a great king and famine in the West, that is, exactly the opposite of what a conjunction of Jupiter and Saturn portended. See Hermann Hunger and Simo Parpola, "Bedeckungen des Planeten Jupiter durch den Mond," *Archiv für Orientforschung* 29/30 (1983/84), pp. 46–49.

3. Heikki Tuori, "The Star of Bethlehem and the Computer," *Uusi Suomi* 8:1 (1976) (in Finnish).

4. More accurately 7/6 B.C.E., since the Babylonian lunar year began at the vernal equinox (March/April).

5. With the establishment of Greek control over the Near East after the conquests of Alexander the Great (fourth century B.C.E.), the most important Babylonian gods became syncretized with Greek ones. Thus Ishtar, the goddess of love and beauty, was equated with Aphrodite; Marduk, the king of gods, was equated with Zeus; Nergal, the god of war, was equated with Ares; and so on. The Greeks also adapted from the Babylonians the idea of associating the leading gods of their pantheon with planets, stars and days of the week. These associations were later taken over by the Romans, who in their turn equated Greek gods with their own.

"While they were eating, Jesus took a loaf of bread, and after blessing it he broke it, gave it to the disciples, and said, 'Take, eat; this is my body.' Then he took a cup, and after giving thanks he gave it to them, saying, 'Drink from it, all of you; for this is my blood of the covenant, which is poured out for many for the forgiveness of sins.' "

(Matthew 26:26-28)

Part VII

THE HOLY GRAIL

At the Last Supper, Jesus shared bread and wine with his disciples and told them to eat and drink of these staples in remembrance of his sacrifice and as a sign of the new covenant. This meal has been reenacted by Christians during the sacrament of the Eucharist for two millennia, and you could say the Last Supper never ended. But what became of the dishes?

Since the Middle Ages, the cup used at the Last Supper has been known as the Holy Grail. Like the lost Ark of the Covenant, this object has proved a powerful and ever-elusive dream for pilgrims, seekers and archaeologists. But as Ben Witherington III shows in the next chapter, the search is misguided, based on a too-literal understanding of something Jesus and the early Christians intended as a metaphor. The cup used at the Last Supper was never important to the early Christians except as a symbol of eternal life. Only in the Middle Ages, when the cult of relics grew, did Christians seek out the physical remains of Jesus' Passion.

CHAPTER 12

The Search for the Holy Grail

Misguided from the Start

Ben Witherington III

———

Most of us remember the dramatic ending of the last Indiana Jones movie, *The Last Crusade*, when good-guy Jones confronts a wicked quester for the Holy Grail in a room full of cups. A Knight Templar is guarding the vessels, some of which are gorgeous, jewel-studded metal items, others rudimentary wooden cups. But which one is the true grail, the cup Jesus shared with his disciples at the Last Supper, the cup that tradition (and the Knight Templar) promises will give eternal life? The wicked quester concludes it must be one of the more ornate cups. He grabs a shining gold vessel, drinks from it—and immediately disintegrates into a lifeless pile of dust. The Knight Templar wryly quips: "He chose poorly."

But is this the only poor choice the wicked quester has made? Or is the whole enterprise of looking for the Holy Grail a poor choice?

The historical search for the Holy Grail seems to have taken place off and on since the Middle Ages. In the late 12th and 13th centuries it was used as a literary device in courtly romances about the spiritual progress of knights. But the searchers have seldom considered our earliest evidence of this elusive cup: the New

Testament. To determine whether such searches for a cup of eternal life might be fertile or futile, we must turn to the Letters of Paul and the Gospels—and not late medieval romances.

The first question to ask these texts is whether there ever was a Holy Grail—a single, special cup used at the Last Supper.

First, regarding the quality of the cup, we can safely dismiss the idea that a chalice, a metal cup, would have been used. We must remember that this meal, according to the Gospels of Matthew, Mark and Luke, took place during the Jewish Passover festival (more on this later), and the normal cup or cups that would have been used at such a meal would have been quite ordinary indeed, not a cup fit for a king. The Gospels offer no suggestion that the host of this meal was wealthy and thus would possess any expensive drinking cups or bowls (which were also commonly used in the first century). It is most likely that the Last Supper cup was carved of wood—quite fitting for a carpenter's last meal—or white chalk, a form of soft limestone that was popular for drinking vessels in first-century Jerusalem.* In either case, it is unlikely, although not impossible, that the cup would have survived the centuries in the way a metal cup might have done. It is even more unlikely that the cup would have any distinguishing markings or design that would allow us to identify it with any certainty or even probability today.

Second is the question of quantity: Was there one communal cup at the Last Supper?

Our earliest record of what happened at the Last Supper is found in Paul's first letter to the Corinthians, written in the early 50s A.D. According to Paul, "After supper [Jesus] took the cup saying, 'This cup is the new covenant in my blood; do this, whenever you drink it, in remembrance of me.' For whenever you eat this bread and drink this cup you proclaim the Lord's death until he comes." The repeated use of the phrase "this cup" may imply a communal cup. The earliest gospel, Mark, seems to make this explicit: "Then he took *the* cup, gave thanks and offered it to them, and they all drank from it" (Mark 14:23). Matthew 26:27 and Luke 22:17 appear to agree; John 13 does not mention a cup at all. So the evidence suggests there was indeed one communal cup that Jesus had the disciples partake

*Yitzhak Magen, "Ancient Israel's Stone Age," *Biblical Archaeology Review*, September/October 1998.

of. Interestingly enough, the text never says that Jesus himself drank from the cup, though this may be implied.[1]

So, we may conclude there was a cup—a Holy Grail, if you will—but it is unlikely that it would have survived or that it would have been in any way distinguishable from the typical cups used in first-century Jerusalem.

Thus far, we have been talking about literal references to the cup in the New Testament. But throughout the Gospels, the term "cup" is used both metaphorically and literally, though seldom are the two types of references considered together. These metaphorical references have been equally important in inspiring the quest for the Holy Grail.

Consider the story of Jesus praying in the Garden of Gethsemane the night before he is to die. In great agony, Jesus throws himself on the ground and asks God to rescue him from his horrible fate. In Mark 14:36 (and parallels), Jesus beseeches God: "Take this *cup* from me." The cup is a metaphor for Jesus' own death.

Compare this to Mark 10:38 where two of the apostles, the sons of Zebedee, ask Jesus for the "box seats" (one at Jesus' right hand, the other at his left) in the kingdom of God. Jesus responds: "Can you drink the cup I drink, or be baptized with the baptism I am baptized with?" Jesus is alluding to his death and resurrection, although the disciples seem to miss the metaphor. They respond rather glibly, "We can."

Why does Jesus associate the "cup" with death? The answer comes from the Hebrew Scriptures, and its many references to drinking from the cup of God's wrath. For example, Psalm 75:8: "In the hand of the Lord is a cup of foaming wine mixed with spices; he pours it out and all the wicked of the earth drink it down to its very dregs." Or Isaiah 51:17: "Awake, awake! Rise up, O Jerusalem, you who have drunk from the hand of the Lord, the cup of his wrath, you who have drained it to its dregs." Lamentations 4:21-22 reads, "Rejoice and be glad, O Daughter of Edom, you who live in the land of Uz. But to you also the cup will be passed; you will be drunk and stripped naked...But, O Daughter of Edom, he will punish your sin and expose your wickedness."

In each case, the cup represents the death that God's wrath or judgment will bring upon sinners. Note that it is always God who offers the cup. Thus, when Jesus asks God to "take this cup" in the Garden of Gethsemane, he is not just shrinking from death, but from a death that is God's punishment for sin.

At the Last Supper, Jesus further transforms this cup metaphor so that the vessel becomes a symbol of both death and redemption. According to Paul, "The Lord Jesus on the night he was betrayed, took bread, and when he had given thanks, he broke it and said, 'This is my body which is for you; do this in remembrance of me.' In the same way, after supper he took the cup saying, 'This cup is the new covenant in my blood; do this, whenever you drink it, in remembrance of me.' For whenever you eat this bread and drink this cup you proclaim the Lord's death until he comes" (1 Corinthians 11:23-26). Similarly, in our earliest gospel account, Mark 14:12-26, Jesus says about the bread, "Take it; this is my body," and about the cup, "This is my blood of the covenant, which is poured out for many."

Scholars have endlessly debated whether or not the Last Supper was a Passover meal, held during the Jewish festival that commemorates the Exodus from Egypt, and especially the night when the angel of death "passed over" the houses of Jews who had put blood on the lintel of their doors (see Exodus 11-12).* In my view it likely was, but it was a Passover meal at which Jesus reinterpreted the traditional meaning of certain aspects of the meal.

In Jewish tradition, various elements of the Passover meal recall specific events of the flight from Egypt. For example, the unleavened bread (*matzoh*) served at Passover represents the bread the Israelites made but did not have time to let rise in their haste to leave Egypt. The Passover lamb represents a substitutionary sacrifice that spares those covered by its blood from the wrath of the death angel sent by God.

Jesus personalizes the Passover meal as a reference to his own coming death and the salvation this will bring. By saying "this is my body ... this is my blood" in the context of the Passover meal, and speaking of a covenant or new covenant, Jesus implies what the Gospel of John, the last gospel to be written, states clearly:

*There appears to be a conflict between the Synoptic Gospels (Matthew, Mark and Luke) and the Gospel of John. See Baruch M. Bokser, "Was the Last Supper a Passover Seder?" *Bible Review* 3:2 (Summer 1987); Jonathan Klawans, "Was Jesus' Last Supper a Seder?" *Bible Review* 17:5 (October 2001); and the dated but still helpful study by Joachim Jeremias, *The Eucharistic Words of Jesus* (London: SCM, 1966).

that Jesus was the new Passover Lamb whose death would take away the sins of the world, by absorbing God's just judgment on sin (John 1:29). The cup at the Last Supper is thus still a cup of God's wrath—a symbol of death as divine punishment for sin—but it is equally a cup of redemption. In offering his cup to his disciples, Jesus is in effect symbolically offering the disciples redemption—the benefit of his death—before he even dies![2]

Jesus intends this meal to be a remembrance meal, just as the Passover meal had been, only now his disciples were to celebrate a new release from slavery and bondage, a new Passover, a new Exodus—involving the release from the bondage of sin for Jesus was indeed to drink the cup of God on the cross.

So what then of the quest for the Holy Grail? The power of the cup at the Last Supper is symbolic. The cup is a vivid reminder of the promise of eternal life. But in the earliest Christian thinking, the cup itself does not provide the elixir of life; that comes only from faith in the death of Jesus. We have no reason from early Christian literature of the first or second centuries to think that Jesus' first followers valued the cup as something other than a symbol. Nor do these early writings offer any hint that the Last Supper cup was saved or preserved. The ongoing search for the Holy Grail is nothing more than an exercise in futility. It is, as the Knight Templar told us in Indiana Jones's *Last Crusade*, a very poor choice indeed.

---

1.   This might be implied by the saying that follows in Mark 14:25, in which Jesus says he will not drink again of the fruit of the vine again until he drinks it new in the kingdom. But even here it is not clear whether he had already committed himself to abstain and so simply passed the cup to the disciples, or not.

2.   This is not the place to get embroiled in the details of the controversy about whether these words are more than symbolic. Suffice it to say that 1) the words about the bread of haste and the bitter herbs and the like in the Passover meal were clearly seen as symbolic, not as literal; 2) the original Aramaic of Jesus' words cannot be understood to mean "This becomes my body, this becomes my blood," as if the ritual was magically transforming the elements into something they had not been previously. Had an early Jewish audience such as Jesus' thought he was talking about his actual physical body and blood they would have run out of the room screaming about cannibalism. 3) The Aramaic probably was "This ... my body" "This ... my blood" since the verb "to be" would have been lacking in that language in such a saying. 4) It is interesting that we get the phrase 'hocus pocus' from the Latin form of Jesus' words *Hoc est meus corpus* ("This is my body").

"When it was evening, there came a rich man from Arimathea, named Joseph, who was also a disciple of Jesus. He went to Pilate and asked for the body of Jesus; then Pilate ordered it to be given to him. So Joseph took the body and wrapped it in a clean linen cloth and laid it in his own new tomb, which he had hewn in the rock. He then rolled a great stone to the door of the tomb and went away."

(Matthew 27:57-60)

Part VIII

THE SHROUD OF TURIN

Locked in a reliquary in the Cathedral of St. John, in Turin, Italy, lies a 14- by 3-foot linen cloth bearing an image of a dead man. Some say the image was created when the cloth was wrapped around Jesus' crucified body. Others claim it is the work of an extremely talented medieval artist. All agree that there is much we do not know about the Shroud of Turin and how, when and why it was created.

In 1978, after a rare public exhibition of the shroud, a team of scientists (called the Shroud of Turin Research Project, or STURP) was invited to examine the cloth. The STURP members returned home to their labs with quantities of photographs, X-rays and sticky-tape samples to study. In the following chapter, Robert A. Wild surveys their mixed findings. Research continued throughout the 1980s, when the cardinal of Turin commissioned three laboratories to perform radiocarbon tests on the shroud. As reported in the article by Suzanne F. Singer, all three labs independently dated the shroud to between 1260 and 1390 A.D. The tests have not convinced everyone, however, as some claim that the shroud's exposure to high temperatures in the 16th century may have skewed the results.

CHAPTER 13

Art, Artifice or Artifact?

Supposed Burial Shroud Probably Made in 14th Century

Robert A. Wild

As both an historian of New Testament times and a Christian believer, I can easily accept the possibility that Jesus' burial cloth might have survived for two millennia. On the other hand, my Christian faith in no way depends on the authenticity of the Shroud of Turin. So I thought I could approach the question of the shroud's authenticity without bias, although I confess to a certain initial skepticism.

Now, after reading several publications on the shroud, most by people who started skeptically as I did and have since come to believe, I am more doubtful than ever that the Shroud of Turin is the burial cloth of Jesus Christ. I suspect that the shroud is either a deliberate forgery or, more innocently, the product of a later devotional art. I say this despite the fact that many questions about the shroud, including the technique by which the image was imposed on it, remain unsolved.

The cloth itself is a strip of linen 14.25 feet long and 3.58 feet wide. The linen is woven in a fine, durable, three-to-one herringbone twill. At some undetermined date a matching strip of linen 3.5 inches wide was attached along one of the long sides of the cloth.

Faintly visible on one side of the cloth are images of the front and back of a human body. These images, described by various modern investigators as "straw yellow" or "sepia yellow" in color, are oriented on the cloth in a head-to-toe fashion: If a human body actually caused the images, it would have to have been placed on its back on one half of the linen fabric. The remaining portion of the cloth would then have to have been drawn up over the head and face and stretched out over the trunk and the legs to form a complete burial shroud. The body is that of a 5-foot-11-inch bearded male Caucasian weighing about 170 pounds.

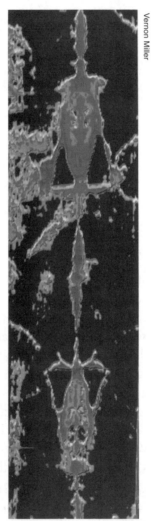

Vernon Miller

The Shroud of Turin bears faint images of the front and back of an unclothed man, about 5 feet 11 inches tall, with long hair and a beard. The man appears to have suffered numerous wounds, some of them leaving what look like bloodstains on the cloth. There is a large cut on his right side and another on his left wrist; there are shoulder abrasions as well as puncture marks on the head and scores of small straight wounds covering the body from the neck down. If the images were produced by a body, that body would have been placed, lying on its back, on the bottom half of the cloth; then the cloth would have been stretched over the top of the body.

The body images reveal wounds and bruises. A number of them are associated with what would appear to be bloodstains, which conform to what we might expect from the gospel accounts of Jesus' crucifixion.

The Biblical texts indicate that Jesus' hands and feet were held fast to the cross by nails (Luke 24:40; John 20:20,25,27; see also

Colossians 2:14). The wounds caused by nails driven through the hands or wrists could account as well for the angular bloodstains that appear on the forearms of the man of the shroud. His right wrist, hidden under the left hand, is not visible, but a blood flow can clearly be seen issuing from the base of the left hand and from both of the victim's feet.

A multitude of small wounds cover the entire body, front and back, from the shoulders down. These conform to the wounds Jesus received when he was scourged by Roman soldiers preparatory to his crucifixion (Matthew 27:26; Mark 15:15; Luke 23:16,22; John 19:1).

According to John's gospel, Jesus was pierced in the side by a Roman soldier's lance (John 19:31-37). The man of the shroud has a wound with a large bloodstain around it at the rib cage on the right side. The dorsal image also shows a flow of blood at this point along the small of the back.

Around the head of the man of the shroud are smaller lesions from which blood has trickled downward. These seem entirely consistent with the wounds inflicted on Jesus when the soldiers who were mocking his supposed kingship pressed a "crown" of sharp thorns upon his head (Matthew 27:29, Mark 15:17; John 19:2).

While all this evidence is clear to anyone who views photographs of the shroud, some investigators believe that they can also discern bruise marks from blows to the face (see Matthew 26:68, 27:30; Mark 14:65, 15:19; Luke 22:63-64; and John 18:22, 19:3), bruises on the shoulders that perhaps would have been caused by the carrying of the cross (see John 19:17), and bruises on the knees that Jesus might have received if he took a fall under the cross's burden.

The history of the shroud can be traced with assurance for only a little more than 600 years. In about 1357, the shroud was exhibited in Lirey, a village near Troyes in northeastern France. The Musée de Cluny in Paris still preserves a pilgrim's medallion from this exhibition. On it appears the first known depiction of the double image of the shroud. The medallion also contains the coats of arms of Geoffrey de Charny and his wife, Jeanne de Vergy, then the owners of the shroud.

The de Charnys retained possession of the shroud until about 1460, when it passed into the hands of the House of Savoy—the family that held legal title to the shroud until 1983. For a time, this family kept the shroud folded up in a silver reliquary chest in the chapel of their castle at Chambéry, a town about 50 miles east of Lyon. There, in 1532, a serious fire broke out. Flames quickly roared through the chapel and almost engulfed the reliquary containing the shroud. A daring intervention by Philip Lambert, counselor to the Duke of Savoy, and two Franciscan priests rescued the already burning reliquary with its precious contents. The reliquary was quickly doused with water to drown the flames. When the box cooled, it was opened to determine the damage to the shroud. The shroud had indeed survived, but a drop of molten silver from the reliquary had set fire to one edge of the shroud, scorching all its 48 folds. In addition, the water that had been poured on the reliquary left stains.

Despite this extensive damage, the body images themselves turned out to be only slightly harmed. During the next two years, a group of nuns repaired the numerous holes with patches. These patches, together with the scorch marks and water stains, are now the most easily visible features of the shroud. It is they, rather than the faint body images, that stand out when the shroud is placed on display.

About 45 years after the fire, the shroud was brought from southeastern France to Turin, in northern Italy. There, in the Royal Chapel of the Cathedral of St. John, it is still preserved, locked away behind grills in a double reliquary container. The outer chest, which is of iron, requires three different keys to open it. One was kept by the former King of Italy, Umberto II.[1] Another belongs to the archbishop of Turin and the third to the cathedral's official custodian.

During the late medieval and Renaissance periods, the shroud was exhibited frequently, both indoors and out. While it aroused considerable popular devotion and interest, the attitude of the Roman Catholic hierarchy toward it tended to be much more reserved. At the time of its first exhibition in 1357, the bishop of Troyes, Henry of Poitiers, claimed the shroud was a fraud, basing his assertion on the testimony of the artist who had made it.

Thirty years later, one of Henry's successors, Pierre d'Arcis, wrote a long letter to Pope Clement VII (which, incidentally, still survives) in which he recalled his predecessor's complaints and indicated that he shared Henry's belief that the shroud was "a product of human handicraft" (*manufactus*) and "an artificial painting or depiction" (*artificialiter depictus*). He pleaded with the pope to end its public display. The pope, replying from Avignon, decided not to withdraw the shroud, but he did place a number of restrictions and reservations on its public display. There was to be no liturgical ceremony or pomp when the shroud was displayed, and on each occasion a priest was to announce to those present "in a loud and intelligible voice, without any trickery, that the aforesaid form or representation [the shroud] is not the true burial cloth (*sudarium*) of Our Lord Jesus Christ but only a kind of painting or picture (*quaedam pictura seu tabula*) made as a form or representation (*in figuram seu repraesentationem*) of the burial cloth."[2]

While later churchmen were more receptive to the shroud—in 1578, for example, Charles Borromeo, then the archbishop of Milan, journeyed to Turin on foot to venerate the shroud—no official affirmation of the shroud's authenticity came from the church.

In 1670 a papal congregation granted an indulgence to those who would come and pray before the shroud. But such individuals would receive this privilege "not for venerating the cloth as the true shroud of Christ but rather for meditating on the Passion [of Jesus]." This kind of official reserve probably explains why in modern times the shroud has been so rarely placed on public display—only about ten times in the last two centuries.

When the shroud went on display in the fall of 1978 to commemorate the 400th anniversary of its arrival in Turin, over three million people attended. The crowds came partly because the shroud had been in the news so frequently during the five years preceding this display. In 1973 a group of European scientists had been allowed to inspect the shroud with a view to providing for its future preservation. Their observations, some favorable to the shroud's authenticity, some not, were widely reported. These reports caught the attention of two U.S. Air Force scientists, John Jackson and Eric Jumper. Jackson and Jumper used equipment designed for creating three-dimensional topographical projections from satellite photographs of the moon and the planets to examine photographs of the shroud. Their surprising discovery was that they could generate an undistorted three-dimensional image of the man of the shroud, a feat that they claimed would be impossible if the shroud were simply an ordinary painting. These findings stimulated interest in the shroud within other segments of the scientific community and led Jackson and Jumper to think seriously of an all-out scientific investigation at the time of the shroud's proposed public display in 1978.

Thus was born the Shroud of Turin Research Project (STURP), a project that eventually included more than 30 physicists, chemists, computer specialists, biophysicists, spectroscopists and experts in photomicroscopy from institutions as varied as the Los Alamos National Scientific Laboratory, the Jet Propulsion Laboratory at the California Institute of Technology and Oceanographic Services, Inc. Some of these scientists clearly were motivated by the chance, as they saw it, to demonstrate by scientific means the truth of the Christian faith, but others, including several agnostics, were attracted by the shroud as a complex puzzle to be solved.

The STURP team never enjoyed any formal institutional sponsorship but depended entirely on its own ability to generate funds and to obtain the use of scientific equipment. Jumper, Jackson and Thomas d'Muhala, the latter on loan from the Nuclear Technology Corporation, proved to be organizational wizards in meeting the many problems of putting together a large and complex scientific expedition that had to operate on a limited budget and within a very tight schedule.

But even their great skills failed when it came to the production of a final joint report. This report, at one time promised for 1980, has not appeared, and deep divisions within the group now make it unlikely that it will ever appear.

We are not, however, without information on the work of the STURP project. Since 1978, three important books about the work have appeared, as well as innumerable articles relating to the shroud.[3] I shall refer to the books as Heller[4] (1983), Tribbe[5] (1983) and Stevenson-Habermast[6] (1981). A fourth book, by Ian Wilson[7] (1978), published before the 1978 scientific study, is in many respects still the most valuable, although naturally one must look to the other three for information based on the 1978 tests.

From these books, it is clear that the scientists have not yet solved the problem of whether the shroud is a first-century artifact. Perhaps it is time for historians, especially Biblical historians, and archaeologists to weigh in with their views, since they offer important perspectives quite different from the physicists' and biologists'. Later in this article, I propose to engage in such a discussion, although naturally against the backdrop of evidence available from what are sometimes exaggeratedly referred to as the exact sciences.

However, the first, and perhaps foremost, problem that calls into question the authenticity of the shroud is the appearance of the bloodstains—even assuming that what appear to be bloodstains are in fact from human blood. On the latter point, Italian specialists who examined the stains in 1973 were unable to obtain positive readings when they tested the supposed bloodstains. Two experts on the 1978 team, John Heller (the author of one of the post-1978 books) and Alan Adler, ran a series of sophisticated experiments on the supposed bloodstains on the shroud and concluded the stains were in fact made by human blood. Heller's book is primarily an account of how the tests were conducted and how he and Adler analyzed the results and reached their conclusions. I was convinced by their evidence that the purported bloodstains were in fact bloodstains.

On the other hand, not everyone has accepted their experimental results. Walter McCrone, the renowned microscopist who first suggested that Yale University's Vinland Map was a forgery, argued that the so-called bloodstains derive from a red iron-oxide earth pigment. McCrone noted that tiny red-orange particles are found everywhere adhering to the fibers of the shroud. McCrone suggested these particles were iron-oxide residue from paint used to create or enhance the body images found on the shroud.

Heller and Adler rejoined that these particles are blood particles abraded from the stain areas on the shroud as it was repeatedly folded and unfolded through the centuries.

The difficulty with McCrone's theories is that none of the scientists with access to the samples from the shroud itself has been able to confirm McCrone's findings by experimentation.

Other investigators have also questioned whether the purported bloodstains are in fact blood. Samuel Pellicori, an optical physicist and spectroscopist who was also a member of the 1978 expedition, observed: "The red color [of the blood caught in the fibers of the shroud] is startlingly reminiscent of recent blood and not at all what one would expect after a minimum of 600 years." For him the color of the bloodstains on the shroud remains "a mystery."[8]

The uniform redness of what purports to be blood on the shroud is, in truth, difficult to explain, especially in light of the intense but variable heat to which the shroud was subjected in the fire of 1532. Within the silver reliquary there was a temperature gradient ranging from about 900 degrees C at the top of the reliquary where the silver began to melt to below 200 degrees C at the bottom of the reliquary where the shroud remained unscorched. Organic substances exposed to such different temperatures would have decomposed, changed color or volatilized at different rates. The absence of such variations from the top of the folded shroud to the bottom suggests that the shroud was not painted with organic pigments, but also raises questions regarding the theory that the purported bloodstains were produced by actual blood.

Nevertheless, on balance, in view of the many tests conducted by Heller and Adler that did prove positive, I am prepared to accept these stains for what they purport to be—human blood.

But that is far from proving the authenticity of the shroud. The problem with the bloodstains is that they are so clear and precise in outline. This is evident even from photographs of the shroud. Not only are the stains very sharply outlined, but the blood frequently takes a downward gravitational course as if it flowed down while Jesus was suspended on the cross. The direction of the blood flow is not what it would have been if the bleeding had occurred while Jesus' body lay in a horizontal position in the tomb. Clear examples of such bloodstains are those running down the forehead and the arms of the man of the shroud.

Those who are convinced of the shroud's authenticity argue that Jesus' body was not washed before burial and that the shroud therefore reflects blood flows that occurred mostly before Jesus' death on the cross. That is a critical element in any argument that the shroud is authentic. As Ian Wilson recognizes: "Only on the view that Jesus was not washed can the authenticity of the Turin Shroud be upheld."[9]

One of the Four Gospels indicates that several women came to Jesus' tomb on the morning after the Sabbath in order to anoint his body (Mark 16:1). From this, various investigators of the shroud conclude that the anointing had been previously omitted because the Sabbath had begun shortly after Jesus' body had been taken down from the cross. They then appeal to a text from the Mishnah* that gives a description of what may legally be done to preserve a corpse on the Sabbath (Mishnah, *Shabbat* 23:5). A dead body may be anointed and washed, says this text, only if the limbs are not moved in the process. With this restriction, argue these investigators, those burying Jesus would have had scruples about anointing him and they would have left his body unwashed as well. To this it may be said, first, that those burying Jesus did not have any scruples about carrying his body some distance, placing it in the tomb, and then rolling a large stone in front of the entrance (Mark 15:46). If they were willing to do all this "work" on the Sabbath, they would not have hesitated to wash and anoint Jesus' body. It is difficult, too, to know if this Mishnaic legislation, which restricts the anointing of a corpse on the Sabbath to such narrow circumstances, accurately reflects normal Jewish practice two hundred years earlier, although the Mishnah certainly incorporated many older traditions. Washing a corpse on the Sabbath may well have been permitted at the time of Jesus' death. In any case, the point of the Mishnaic prescription is that actions needed to preserve a corpse for decent burial, actions such as washing the body, are so important that they take priority over Sabbath rest. Since even the Gospel of Mark says nothing about omitting such customary action, it is safer to suppose that Jesus' body was washed on the evening after his death.

But even if we accept as a fact that Jesus' dead body remained unwashed when he was laid in the tomb, we must then also suppose, given the fact that the bloodstains are precisely defined, that

*The *Mishnah* (from the Hebrew word, to "repeat") is a body of Jewish oral law, specifically, the collection of oral laws compiled by Rabbi Judah the Prince in the second century.

the nails were pulled from Jesus' hands and feet and that his body was then taken down from the cross, carried some distance to the tomb, and laid upon the linen shroud, all without smearing or rubbing the bloodstains! This, it seems to me, stretches credulity to the breaking point.

If the writer of the Gospel of John is historically correct in reporting that a very large quantity of spices was wrapped with the burial garments around Jesus' body (John 19:39-40), such materials would almost certainly have smeared and distorted the bloodstains.

In their book, Stevenson and Habermas recognize that where the blood still remained wet around the wounds, the linen would have become loosely attached. Eventually separating the fabric from such areas, if this occurred in any normal way, would have been like removing a bandage; further deformation of the bloodstains would surely have occurred. They therefore appeal to a miraculous cause: The images on the shroud were produced by a flash of light at the moment of Jesus' resurrection from the dead. But appealing to a miracle is not necessary in this case; a rational explanation would suffice.

Tribbe is one of the few writers who makes an effort to face these issues: He recognizes that the bloodstains would surely have been smeared when Jesus was taken from the cross. He therefore postulates that Jesus' body was washed before burial and that the stains on the shroud were from blood that flowed from the wounds after Jesus' body was laid to rest in the tomb. One problem with this suggestion is that it requires us to suppose that even the superficial wounds continued to bleed for a very considerable time after Jesus' death, a most dubious medical possibility. An even greater difficulty with this explanation of the clear and precisely outlined bloodstains is that if they reflect blood that flowed after Jesus was laid in the tomb, the blood flowed up to more elevated portions of the body, instead of down. In short, the blood flows do not run in the right direction if they occurred while Jesus' body lay on its back.

In these circumstances, Tribbe is forced to resort to an appeal to a "paranormal spiritual event."[10]

My own religious faith certainly allows for the possibility of such miracles. But I am most hesitant to affirm such a miracle when a natural explanation suffices. In this case, it is far more likely that we have caught an artist or forger in a simple mistake. Given the findings of Heller and Adler, we may assume that this artist (or forger) used real blood in creating the various stains.

However, Heller and Adler make no claim that the blood on the shroud dates to the first century rather than to the 15th century. Indeed the blood they used as a control in the tests was Heller's own blood, with which they stained a piece of 16th-century Spanish linen. This they assumed to be comparable to blood from any previous period.

Thus the bloodstains, not actually demonstrated to be first-century blood, present a series of problems related to the fact that their outline is so clear and precise and that they flow in the wrong direction if they occurred while Jesus lay in the tomb.

Other aspects of the physical depiction of the man of the shroud also arouse suspicion. Take the simple fact that the face and hands stand out with particular emphasis. Many other anatomical features, on the other hand, are not clearly delineated. Some apologists explain this by saying that the more elevated portions of Jesus' body were imprinted more clearly on the shroud. This, however, fails to explain why such areas as the chest and the toes are defined poorly or not at all. More probably it is art rather than nature (or miracle) that explains why the face and hands stand out so clearly, for these are the bodily features that habitually receive prominence in artistic portraits.

In addition, many features of the body reflect a too "appropriate"—and therefore "artistic"—modesty. The buttocks are only faintly outlined and the genital region is altogether invisible. If the shroud actually preserves an imprint of Jesus' naked body as he lay in the tomb, we would expect that imprint to have formed without hesitancy and reserve. The apparent absence of any navel could even be an effort to remind the viewer of the teaching of the virginal birth of Jesus.

The treatment of the hands loosely joined at the pelvic region presents special problems. Recent research by two scholars, Rachel Hachlili and Ann Killebrew, indicates that in this period in the Jericho and Jerusalem areas, people were customarily buried with their arms at their sides.[11] It is true, however, that at Qumran (where the Dead Sea Scroll community lived in the first century

A.D.), burials were excavated in which the hands seemed to be joined on the torso.[12] However, this burial posture from Qumran is also known from the 14th century.[13]

In any event, neither of these examples can be said to attest to the covering of the genitals with the joined hands. In a relaxed position, a man's joined hands will not cover his genitals if he lies on his back. He will reach the genital area with his hands only by stretching his arms downward. The body on the shroud, however, is relaxed; the elbows extend out beyond the body as though resting on the surface of the tomb. On a dead man's body, joined hands will cover the genital region only if the elbows are propped up on the body and the wrists tied together so as to hold the hands and arms in place. The relaxed arrangement of the body on the shroud rejects this possibility.

To depict a relaxed body on which joined hands cover the genital area requires several anatomical oddities that are conveniently provided on the shroud. The fingers of the right hand are extremely long; the index finger, for example, is at least 5 inches long. The right forearm also appears to be several inches longer than the left. (Because the elbow areas were damaged in the fire of 1532, we cannot be absolutely certain about this.) Only these improbable elongations allow the right hand to cover the genital area. Thus is modesty preserved. This is artistry, not the brute reality of actual death.

Jesus' face as depicted on the shroud also gives me difficulties. It looks very much as we would expect it to look in any medieval or modern portrait. Christians of the second, third, and fourth centuries who painted pictures and carved statues of Jesus had no information about Jesus' exact physical appearance, and their images of him show very great variety. At times he is beardless with short hair; at other times beardless with long hair; at still other times he has a short beard and short hair, and sometimes he is depicted with the more familiar long hair and full beard. An example of this last type, a mid-fourth century portrait of Christ found at Rome in the Catacomb of Commodilla, is rather close in type to our own 20th-century depictions.

Beyond this, however, these early Christians were more interested in portraying the inner nature of Jesus than his bodily appearance. Christ as the Good Shepherd often is a more youthful figure with shorter hair, Christ the Lawgiver usually resembles contemporaneous depictions of Roman emperors, and Christ as the True Teacher of Wisdom has the mature years and full beard proper to philosophers and teachers in late Roman times. Since a full beard was also a symbol of sovereign divinity—gods like Zeus and Sarapis were always shown with such beards—artists increasingly depicted Jesus with a beard to make manifest his own divine nature and his equality with God the Father. From the late fourth century onwards, Jesus is usually, but not always, depicted with long hair parted in the center and a full beard.

This tendency to settle upon a single quasicanonical image for Jesus was accelerated by a general preference in late Roman and Byzantine times for schematic portraits. Such portraits, whether of emperors, Christian saints, or Christ himself, made use of a few fixed symbols to identify with clarity the individual depicted. Often a characteristic arrangement of facial hair helped serve this purpose. To argue, as some proponents of the shroud's authenticity do, that the image of Jesus' face seen on the shroud gave rise to the conventional depiction of Jesus employed in Byzantine and Western European art is to ignore the impact of broader cultural and artistic trends occurring in late antiquity. In any case, the pre-14th-century history of the shroud is far too obscure to justify such a conjecture. A far more likely explanation of the "typical" character of the shroud's portrayal of Jesus is that a forger or devotional artist would naturally tend to copy a conventional likeness. Indeed, the forked beard of the man of the shroud suggests a medieval date since this type of beard occurs only infrequently in earlier depictions of Christ. In short, the face of Jesus on the shroud shows clear links with known artistic patterns. If in some amazing way we could obtain a genuine photograph of Jesus, his face would probably look very different from any of our images of him, since these all derive from the conceptualizations and conventions of art and theology.[14]

Suspicions are also aroused when we attempt to compare the depiction on the shroud with the accounts of Jesus' suffering, death and burial found in the Gospels. Certain features of the shroud image, such as the wounds in the hands and feet and the marks of the scourging, are in accord with all four of the evangelists' accounts. But other features do not enjoy this same uniform attestation. To cite just two examples, only the Gospel of John reports that Jesus' side was pierced with a lance (John 19:31-37), and the Gospel of Luke gives no indication whatever that Jesus was crowned with thorns prior to his crucifixion. Dealing with such problems is not, of course, a matter of counting up references. Luke almost surely had quite definite reasons for deliberately passing over in silence the crowning with thorns, and John certainly could have had access to evidence unavailable to the other evangelists. But if in assessing the shroud, someone points with enthusiasm to the wound in the figure's side as showing clear agreement with the gospel evidence (in reality only with that found in the Gospel of John), this person must then explain why he or she does not accept other evidence from that same source that also is not in harmony with the other Gospels. An investigator cannot just pick and choose a set of details from the different gospel accounts that best accords with the evidence seen on the shroud. Such a procedure ignores problems posed by the gospel evidence and indeed tacitly assumes that the shroud is genuine. Since a later artist or forger could have worked with one eye attentively turned to the Biblical text, the gospel evidence must be scrutinized with care to see if indeed it supports the authenticity of the shroud. In fact, this evidence raises some problems.

Although all four Gospels describe Jesus' burial, they do not agree in all details. According to the Synoptic Gospels (Matthew 27:59; Mark 15:46; Luke 23:53), Joseph of Arimathea wrapped Jesus in a *sindon,* that is, a large linen cloth, and then laid him in the tomb. The shroud's defenders equate this with the shroud itself. The Gospel of John describes a different bodily wrap: "They then took the body of Jesus and wrapped it with the spices in linen cloths (*othoniois* [a plural noun]) as is the Jewish burial custom" (John 19:40). This same gospel adds that after Jesus' resurrection, Peter and the "Beloved Disciple" saw the linen cloths (*othonia* [plural]) lying in the tomb and, in addition, saw a separate cloth called a *soudarion,* probably a wrapping for the face (John 20:5-7). In short, John reports that Jesus' body was wrapped not in one but in several cloths.

If a *soudarion* was used to cover Jesus' face, the shroud for his corpse could not possibly bear an image of the face, for the face would have been separated from the shroud by this *soudarion*.

Some suggest that the *soudarion* was probably only a chin strap designed to hold shut the jaws of a deceased person (compare John 11:44). This may well be correct. If so, the use of such a *soudarion* in the burial of Jesus would have permitted the image of his face to appear on the shroud. Initially, some investigators of the shroud thought they could detect such a chin strap in photographs of the shroud. Then, a new series of photographs taken in 1978 showed that the supposed strap at the sides of the face was actually an irregularity in the weave of the linen fabric that earlier photographic reproductions had picked up and enhanced; the blank space found at the crown of the head between the frontal and dorsal images was not caused by the knotted portion of a chin strap, as previously believed, but was simply a blank space. If a chin strap was part of Jesus' grave wrappings, it is not to be seen in the shroud. Proponents of the shroud readily accept as historical the account of the lance wound reported in John 19—and only there. They should be equally ready to accept the *soudarion* of chapter 20 or be prepared to offer strong reasons for rejecting this tradition. The evidence of the shroud itself allows for no *soudarion*, whether a head covering or a chin strap.

Moreover, as we have seen, John's gospel indicates that Jesus' body was wrapped in several linen cloths (*othonia*). This too is a problem for the shroud. Some have attempted to interpret *othonia* as a collective singular in order to conform the account in John to the language of the other three Gospels (*sindon*). But it is much more likely that the author of John was referring to more than one cloth.[15] Some suggest that the various cloths designated by the term *othonia* were placed on top of one another, so the innermost one would be *the* shroud, but such an arrangement of the cloths remains a pure conjecture. While this hypothesis at least offers a possible solution for John's use of *othonia*, the shroud shows no sign whatever of the *soudarion* that John clearly states was part of Jesus' grave wrappings.

One feature of the shroud may even rest on later Christian tradition rather than on gospel evidence, a situation that would, if true, render the shroud particularly suspect. Defenders of the shroud's authenticity interpret marks on the shoulders and knees of the man of the shroud as bruises and abrasions. The bruises on the shoulders occurred, they say, when Jesus carried his cross (John 19:17). The cuts and abrasions on the knees resulted from falls, falls that caused Jesus' executioners to force Simon of Cyrene to carry Jesus' cross (Matthew 27:32; Mark 15:21; Luke 23:26). However, it is not quite so easy to combine the gospel evidence to produce this version of events. Probably for theological reasons, John insists that Jesus carried his own cross. He makes no mention of any help from Simon. On the other hand, the passage in Mark 15:20-21 can be interpreted as saying that Jesus never carried the cross at all.

Since John almost certainly had a deliberate purpose in downplaying Jesus' weakness and need for help, Simon's assistance seems most probable as an historical occurrence. Yet the fact remains that none of the Gospels gives any reason why Simon was forced to march along with the cross. Later Christian tradition supplied a theory to fill this Biblical lacuna: Jesus fell one or more times with the cross and so needed help. This interpretation then became an entrenched part of the Christian imagination and piety, appearing for example in the later representations of the Stations of the Cross. If the shroud indeed records the bruises from such falls, this is in conformity not with evidence from the New Testament but with later Christian tradition. This is what we would expect from a later artisan but not from an authentic object.

Some investigators have sought to demonstrate the shroud's authenticity by appeals to detailed features that could not have been known or understood by a 14th-century forger. None of these efforts to establish the shroud's authenticity has been successful or convincing.

For example, Professor Francis Filas, S.J., of Loyola University in Chicago thought he saw coins on Jesus' eyes. Then, in the late 1970s, a Jewish burial from shortly after the time of Jesus was excavated near Jericho. The investigator, Rachel Hachlili, initially suggested that two coins found in the skull had originally been placed on the dead man's eyes and then later had dropped into the skull.[16] Filas naturally saw this as strong supporting evidence for his theory.

However, further work on the Jericho site made it clear to Hachlili that her initial assessment of the data had been premature. She went on to discover a second skull with a single coin in it. Since one coin will not cover two eyes, it seemed more probable that these rare examples of coins in association with skulls— at Jericho only two instances out of 192 burials investigated—represent a Jewish adaptation of the Greek custom of putting one or more coins in the mouth of the deceased. That person would then be able to pay "Charon's fee," that is, the cost of a boat trip across the River Styx into the Underworld.[17] Thus, the placement of coins on the eyes of the deceased remains unattested in Jewish practice in the first century A.D.

In the case of the shroud, however, Filas believes he can even detect the kinds of coins that were placed on Jesus' eyes. They are small bronze *lepton* coins minted during the middle years of Pontius Pilate's procuratorship in Judea (29-32 A.D.). Filas has produced shadowy photographs of one of these coins in support of his contention.[18] Admittedly, it is most unlikely that a later artist or forger would have known of such coins. But are these particular coins actually there in the image on the shroud?

Filas's claim that the coins are visible highlights another problem with many claims by those who support the shroud's authenticity: The image of the shroud is very faint. For the naked eye the optimal viewing distance is about 6 to 10 feet away; closer up the image blurs and dissolves. The eye of the camera, on the other hand, tends to enhance the actual light-dark contrasts and to produce a clearer-than-life image. But the photographic image that clarifies can also deceive. Many tend to see in the photographs not what is there but what they want to see. We have already noted that the chin strap thought to be visible in earlier photographs of the shroud disappeared in the 1978 photographs. Earlier photographs seemed to indicate, too, that Jesus wore his hair in the form of a pigtail. This also disappeared in the 1978 photographs. Filas's claim that he sees two particular coins on the shroud is subject to the same uncertainty.

A final problem with the shroud's authenticity is its lack of any convincing history prior to the 14th century. More than half of Ian Wilson's book is an effort to reconstruct such a history. But most of it is sheer, unsupportable conjecture. Wilson may have done an imaginative job with limited scraps of evidence, but Heller is certainly correct in calling Wilson's history of the shroud "a fanciful collage."

Given all these various difficulties, especially the implausibility of the bloodstains, the iconographic and anatomical irregularities, the anomalies with respect to the Biblical evidence, and the early history—or lack of it—of the shroud, I find the authenticity of this object quite suspect. On the other hand, no one has provided a completely satisfactory explanation of how the image on the shroud was produced. In the absence of such an explanation, despite massive modern scientific efforts to produce one, the inference is drawn that it was somehow produced by a miracle.

Two characteristics of the image are especially puzzling: As early as 1898 it was noted that highlights of the image are dark, and recessed areas are light, producing what can best be compared to a photographic negative, rather than a positive. Second, as I mentioned above, John Jackson and Eric Jumper discovered that they could produce a more or less undistorted three-dimensional image from a computer analysis of the 1931 photographs of the shroud. This meant that a direct correlation exists between the intensity of color at any point on the shroud and the proximity or distance of the cloth from whatever object produced this color. The lighter the color, the further the cloth from the object. Attempts to analyze a two-dimensional portrait in a similar fashion produce a severely distorted image.

A final miracle-suggesting feature of the shroud is that the image could not have been painted on it. The shroud image blurs and fades when viewed from closer than 6 feet. It is very unlikely that a painter could paint an image that would have this effect. Such a painter would even have had trouble seeing the work as it progressed! Moreover, both earlier studies and the 1978 investigation of the shroud indicate that there are no signs of brush marks or other "directional" strokes that would indicate that the shroud had been painted.

While obviously I cannot prove it, my impression is that an artist (or forger) scorched a linen cloth with a properly heated statue or, more likely, a pair of bas-reliefs, using whole blood to nants of their old friendship. Would he expect some affection or commitment from her when he made the crib? Somehow she knew that he was only doing it because he saw her as his future wife. Anita was certain that Amos had something to do with that.

Eli glanced at her. "What kind of wood do you like?"

"I'm not certain. Would it be painted?"

"You could have it painted if you want, but real wood-lovers like to see the color and the grain of the wood."

"That makes sense. Whatever you think is best."

He tipped his hat back on his head. "You've got to have some opinions, Anita."

Anita hoped she wasn't making him angry. She had become careful what she said around Amos lately, but she excused him because he was her brother. Anita certainly didn't want a husband, or even a potential husband, that she had to worry about offending or upsetting. Anita shook her head at that thought. Everyone was pushing her to find another man, and now she found she'd been entertaining the idea.

"Do you feel okay? Do you want me to stop the buggy a while?" Eli asked.

"*Nee,* I'm okay, *denke.* I was just thinking we could look at the timber when we're at the lumber yard, and then I can say which one I like."

"*Nee.* It's rough wood; you won't be able to tell anything from that. I'll take you to a furniture store where you can see all the different kinds of wood."

"That sounds *gut.*"

He stopped the buggy at a furniture store. Anita was quick to get out of the buggy before he got to the other side to help her down. It was a large Amish furniture store, which hadn't been there when Anita had lived in the area. "This building wasn't even here a few years ago."

"*Jah*, it seems as though it's fairly new." He pushed the door open for her, and she walked through. As they walked down the aisles of furniture, Eli pointed out all the different varieties of wood.

When they rounded the end of one of the aisles, Anita saw someone who looked like Simon. She focused more intently and saw that it was Simon. "Let's look over this way," she said pointing in the other direction. She did not want to let Simon see her with Eli.

"Good idea. There are cribs over there and you can see the different styles."

Anita made herself concentrate on choosing a crib that looked nice to her, when she heard a familiar voice behind her.

"Hello, Anita."

She swung around to see Simon. "Simon, I didn't know you were here."

Simon stared at Eli and Eli stared back at him.

"Simon, this is..." Anita's mind went blank as she searched for her friend's name.

Eli put his hand out. "I'm Eli Smith."

"I'm Simon, Hannah's *bruder.*" They shook hands.

"*Jah,* Hannah's *bruder,*" Anita mumbled.

"Is this what you had planned today?" Simon asked staring intently at Anita.

She knew she had put off their outing to choose paint for his house, and hadn't told him she was going somewhere with Eli.

"*Jah.* Eli's been kind enough to offer to make me a crib. He's showing me designs and all the different types of wood."

Anita was just about to ask Simon what had brought him into the store, but before she could say anything further, Simon said, "I'll leave you both to it, then." He nodded to Eli before he walked away.

Anita stood open-mouthed and watched Simon walk away.

"So that's Hannah's younger *bruder?*"

Anita nodded. "Do you remember him?"

"Barely. He was so much younger. He's much younger than both of us. I'm sure he would've been just a *boppli* when you married Joshua."

"He's only six years younger."

"Is there anything between the two of you? Tell me now so I don't waste any more of my time."

Anita studied his face. Could he tell that she was genuinely fond of Simon? She had to cover up the feelings that she didn't want to admit to herself. *"Jah,* you're right. He's much younger than both of us."

"I'm sorry, Anita, I just can't do this."

"Do what?"

"I can't make you a crib when you've got your eyes on someone else. I put a lot of effort into my furniture. I can't make it for you now."

Anita looked down at the ground. "Whatever you think is best. I guess we should head home."

Eli said nothing and walked out of the store in front of her. He didn't even hold the door open for her. When she reached the buggy he was already sitting in the driver's seat with his hands on the reins.

It was a tense trip home, and it was even tenser when they arrived home. With Amos out working in the fields and Hannah at the candy store, it was just the two of them.

"Would you like a cup of tea or *kaffe?*"

He looked up from his seated position on the couch, and lowered the Amish newspaper he'd been reading. "I can't do this any more." Eli jumped up, and placed the newspaper on the couch behind him.

"Do what?"

"You've changed, Anita. You're not the same girl I used to know. You're setting yourself up for heartache if you think that man we saw today would ever be interested in you."

"I haven't got my eyes on anybody, Eli. I keep telling everybody that I'm not ready for anything at this time in my life."

"That's not the impression your *bruder* gave me."

"Amos?"

"Seems I've come all this way for nothing. When Amos told me you needed a husband, I thought I could come in and be a *vadder* to your child, and husband to you, but you haven't welcomed me. I'm too old to chase you, or try to win you from another man."

Anita shrugged her shoulders reaching for words. Nothing came to mind.

"I'm going to pack my things, and then call a taxi." He left her, and trudged up the stairs.

"Where you going?" she called after him.

"Back home."

Anita collapsed onto the couch, hoping

that Amos wouldn't blame her for Eli's sudden disappearance. But, in a way, she was glad to be relieved of the pressure. Now, with him gone and not making a crib for the baby, she wouldn't have to worry about feeling obligated toward him.

Fifteen minutes later, Eli threw his suitcases down at the front door and strode to the barn. Anita guessed he was calling for a taxi to take him to the bus stop. When he came out of the barn, he waited on the porch. Anita was too scared of his anger to join him.

When the taxi came, Eli opened the front door to retrieve his suitcases, and then closed the door heavily behind him. Anita watched through the window as he got into the taxi.

When the taxi was out of sight, Anita was flooded with a sense of peace and relief. Although she didn't like seeing anybody upset, a heavy load had been lifted from her.

She walked upstairs and looked at the crib in Sam's room. *There's nothing wrong with that. That'll do nicely.* On her way back downstairs, she wondered if she'd also upset Simon. She deliberately hadn't told him what she was doing when he wanted to take her to look at the paint. Would he see her not telling him that she had a prior appointment with Eli as being deceptive? Would he still come by to collect her tomorrow as they had arranged? Anita hoped that he would.

When afternoon came, with Eli gone, it was left to Anita to collect Hannah from work.

Hannah was surprised to see Anita driving the buggy. Before they fetched the boys from Hannah's mother's house, Anita told Hannah everything that had happened that day.

CHAPTER 15

And the peace of God, which passeth all understanding, shall keep your hearts and minds through Christ Jesus.
Philippians 4:7

"What do you mean, Eli's gone?" Amos bellowed.

"Can't you see she's upset, Amos?" Hannah said.

Anita was helping Hannah mash vegetables for the boys' dinner. "He left and I don't know why. He didn't really say. He seemed to think I needed a husband and when I told him I wasn't interested, he became angry. He called a taxi and left." Anita shrugged her shoulders. She'd left out the part about running into Simon in the furniture store. The part she left out was her private business, and she didn't see why her younger brother should know every single thing about her life.

"Just like that? He just walked out, did he?

"*Jah.* That's right. You can ask him yourself. I didn't ask him to leave."

"I'll give him a couple of days to get home, and then I'll call him and find out for myself."

Hannah rounded her shoulders. "As you wish."

Amos stared at her as though he knew there was more to the story than what she was telling him.

Anita looked at Hannah. "Did you have a good day at work?"

Before Hannah could answer, Amos butted in, "You've surely talked about that on the way home in the buggy." Amos stood up from the kitchen table, and stomped out of the kitchen.

"He's upset," Hannah said.

Anita raised her eyebrows. "I can see that."

Ben and Sam were sitting at their small table. Hannah passed the boys a cooked carrot each to munch on while they were waiting on their mashed vegetables.

When Anita put the bowls of food in front of the boys, she said to Hannah,

"I need to go and speak to Amos about something." Anita walked out of the kitchen and sat in front of Amos.

He closed his paper up and looked at her.

"It's your fault you know."

Amos drew his eyebrows together. "What is?"

"It's your fault for telling a lie that I was interested in finding a husband. You know that's not true."

Amos looked away from her. "That's because you don't know what's good for you."

"What's good for me is to have a peaceful life, at least until my *boppli* comes into the world. I don't need to keep fighting you about this; I'm not interested in finding another husband. Joshua has only been gone a few months." Anita looked up to the ceiling and blinked rapidly to stop the tears from falling.

Amos stared at her and his mouth turned down at the corners. "I'm only trying to help you. If I don't help you, who else will?"

"I appreciate you wanting to help me, but can you wait to ask me if I want your help with something before you act next time?"

He gradually smiled. "I can do that."

"That'll make me feel much better."

He nodded, and then asked, "When do you go to see the midwife next?"

"I think I need to see her next Wednesday, and then after that, I see her weekly."

"She'll have to start coming here. You can't go driving over those bad roads by yourself."

There he was again being overprotective, but this time he was right, the roads were bad. She didn't want be stuck out on those roads again. "She did say at the later stages she'd come here"

"So she should. I'll take you there next week, and then we need to make sure that she comes here to see you."

"Denke, Amos."

Anita pushed herself to her feet, and went back into the kitchen to help Hannah with the dinner.

CHAPTER 16

*And walk in love, as Christ also hath loved us,
and hath given himself for us an offering and a
sacrifice to God for a sweetsmelling savour.*
Ephesians 5:2

The next morning, Anita walked into the kitchen just after day-break. Hannah was already baking bread, and the two boys munched on something at their small table. "Amos has already left?" Anita asked.

"*Jah.* He wanted to get an early start."

"Eli was meant to help him today; that makes me feel bad."

"It was Eli's choice to leave. Do you have plans for the day?" Hannah asked Anita.

Anita sat down at the table wondering if Hannah knew her brother was coming by to take her somewhere. "Simon did mention that he might come by. He said he was going to take me somewhere, but I forget where."

Hannah laughed. "You're getting forgetful. I was like that during both my pregnancies."

"Were you?"

Hannah nodded, and Anita felt a little better. She was normally not forgetful; neither did she usually cry over small things.

IT WAS mid-morning when Anita heard a horse and buggy making its way to the house. Her heart beat faster when she looked out the window to see that it was Simon. She was happy he hadn't been put off by her not being entirely truthful about the previous day.

"Sounds like he's here," Hannah called to Anita.

"I'm coming." Anita hurried to her room, placed her over-bonnet on, pulled her black shawl off the peg, and then came back into the main house. Anita kissed the boys, and said goodbye to Hannah. When she opened the front door, she came face-to-face with Simon.

"Hello, Anita. You're very rosy-cheeked today."

"Hello. I think it's the cold." She suddenly felt nervous and excited at the same time.

Simon looked into the house at Hannah, and gave her a wave. He called out to Hannah, "I'll come back later to play with the boys." He looked at Anita. "You ready?"

Anita nodded, and then they made their way out to his buggy.

Try as she might, Anita could not remember where he had said he was taking her. She hoped he'd mention where they were going soon.

As they traveled down the long driveway, Simon asked. "Eli helping Amos today?"

"Eli and I had a bit of a falling out, I'm afraid."

He whipped his head around to look at her. "What happened?"

"I upset him."

He was silent for a while before he said, "I find it hard to believe that you could upset anyone."

Anita grunted. "I think I've upset a few people since I've been here."

"Let me guess, one - Amos, and two – Fran?"

Anita giggled.

Simon took his eyes off the road for an instant to glance over at her. "Am I right?"

"I don't know if I've upset Fran too much, but you're right about Amos."

"Now tell me seriously, what did you do to upset Eli?"

"The whole situation was awkward. He insisted on making a crib for my *boppli* even though Hannah's got a perfectly good crib that she offered to loan me. I was put in a position where I couldn't say 'no.' Then he seemed a little annoyed that I didn't know what kind of wood I wanted or what style I wanted. I'm no expert on that kind of thing." Anita raised her hands in the air.

"And that's when he suggested taking you to the furniture store?"

"*Jah* that's right."

"And you didn't want him to make it because you didn't want to feel obligated to him?"

"That's exactly right." He seemed to understand how she felt, just like her friends back home in Ohio would. She missed her friends terribly. Back home she was always visiting her friends, or they were visiting her. They lived in out of each other's homes. She was happy to live with Amos and Hannah now, and not by herself. It was nice at night to know that there was someone else in the house. She had spent too many nights at home after Joshua had departed, alone with her grief and battling morning sickness, and they had been the worst nights she'd ever had.

Simon broke through her daydreams. "I hope you've given a lot of thought to the colors you're to choose today."

That's when Anita remembered. She was to help him choose paint for his house. "To be truthful, I haven't given any thought to it, at all."

"At least you're honest. Do you know how many shades of white there are?"

"*Nee,* I don't. How many are there?"

"There are about sixty different shades of white, so I'd hate to think how many different shades of cream there'd be. And then after we choose the color, we need to make the decision whether it's going to be flat, gloss, or semi-gloss. Then there's under-paint, over-paint, and the list goes on." Simon glanced over at her and smiled.

"Over-paint? Is that the same as normal paint?"

He shrugged, and then shook his head. "I'm no paint expert."

"I can see how difficult that would be; no wonder you need me to help you."

He wagged a finger at her. "And I'm trusting you to do a good job."

"I'll do my very best."

When they arrived at the paint store,

Anita was pleased that Simon rushed to help her down from the buggy.

They browsed through the paint cards, and then Anita decided on a color. "Do you think you should try a small portion of it on your wall first?"

"Is that what people do?" Simon asked.

"Only if it's an important decision for you. Or, if you're not sure about it."

Simon looked down at the sample paint card in his hand. "I think that'll do fine, and they tell me for walls it's best to choose a flat paint."

Anita nodded. Before long, the paint had been mixed, and Simon was loading two large cans into the back of the buggy.

He looked back at Anita. "You know you have to help me paint, don't you?"

Anita shook her head and put both hands on her tummy. "You'll be waiting a while if you want me to help you. Besides, I didn't say I'd help you paint."

"Fair enough. You'll have to come and watch me while I paint, then."

She shook her head. "Amos wouldn't approve."

Simon chuckled. "You're right about that, I guess."

"How about I come and look at it after you've painted it?"

Simon pulled a sad face. "I suppose that'll have to do. I'll tell you what, I'll let you get out of painting if you agree to have lunch with me right now."

"I could do with something to eat," Anita said.

SIMON TOOK them to a diner on the edge of town. They sat in the very back booth and looked through the menus. "Are you hungry?"

"I'm always hungry lately. Only thing is I

can't eat too much because I get heartburn. The midwife said I have to eat little bits, and often."

After the waitress took their order, Simon stared at Anita.

Anita laughed. "What is it that you're looking at?"

He laughed too. "Nothing."

"You can't laugh at me and then just say 'nothing.' Tell me what's so funny."

"I was just thinking about the situation your *bruder* got you into with Eli."

"I don't know if that's anything to laugh about." Anita grimaced. "He put me in a bad position. It was very embarrassing and probably more so for poor old Eli."

"Have you told your *bruder* how you feel?"

"I had a good talk with him last evening. He seemed to understand how I feel."

"Seemed to?" Simon cocked his head to one side.

"I'm confident he understands."

"Well, both you and Hannah must be wearing him down."

"He does have very definite opinions about things. So, when are you going to start painting?"

"I think I'll start tonight."

"Wouldn't it be better to wait for the warmer weather?"

"*Nee.* We always get busy at work in the summer months. And it doesn't matter too much if it takes a while to dry." He smiled and his eyes sparkled. "I'm in the big house all on my own."

Anita giggled when she remembered what Fran had said. "Fran seemed quite concerned that it's only you in that big house. Do you want me to have a word with her? She'd most likely love to write out a list for you as well."

Simon raised his hands. "Please don't."

Anita stared at him and wondered if he knew that many girls liked him. Fran had said that quite a few girls had come to her house in tears because he never gave them any attention.

"What are you thinking about? You've got that far-away look in your eyes."

"I was just thinking that it must be hard to be a bishop and have to listen to everybody's problems."

"Did you tell him your problems?"

Anita's eyes grew wide as she tried to recall exactly what she'd talked to the bishop about. "When I went to visit the bishop, we only talked for five minutes before he was called away. The rest of the time I spoke to Fran. That's when she gave me the list."

"That's right, and you tasted her chocolate cake. Did you ever get that recipe from her?"

"*Nee.* I haven't asked her about it again, but I have tried various cake recipes to try to make one that tastes the same."

"Any success?"

"Nowhere near it."

"Your big mistake was not getting the recipe right away when she said she'd give it to you."

Anita shrugged her shoulders. "I can't turn back the clock."

The waitress placed their plates in front of them.

Anita stared down at the burger and fries on the over-sized plate. "I don't think I'll be able to get through all of this."

Simon picked up his burger with both hands. "Aren't you eating for two?"

"I've been extremely hungry, but this is far too much. You might have to help me out with this lot."

Simon had just taken a mouthful of burger, so he nodded his head.

When Simon drove Anita home that afternoon, Simon walked into the house with Anita. When Amos saw him, he grunted.

Simon said he had things to do and made an excuse to leave.

Anita wasn't happy with her brother, but because she knew her brother felt bad about Eli leaving, she didn't say anything to him about being so rude.

CHAPTER 17

This is the day which the LORD hath made; we will rejoice and be glad in it.
Psalm 118:24

It was weeks later, and the midwife had visited Anita at the house.

"All's well with the *boppli?*" Amos asked after Dora had left.

"*Jah*, everything is going fine. And she'll

be coming to see me every few days until the birth, since it's so close."

"*Gut.*"

Anita thought about her younger brothers who had left the community. She hadn't seen them in years. She wondered whether they had wives and children, or had remained unmarried. There had been no word from them. It hurt her that they hadn't bothered to keep in touch. She didn't know where they were. They could've called to their parents' old house, or could have written. She glanced over at Amos wondering if he ever thought about his older brothers.

"Simon's coming to dinner," Amos said suddenly.

"*Jah,* he is. I'm glad you two have sorted out your differences."

Amos stared ahead. "It's sometimes not easy to get along with *familye.*"

Anita heard Hannah come back into the house through the back door. She walked into the kitchen and saw Hannah with a bundle of vegetables. "She said everything looks good, Hannah."

"I'm glad. And the space we made for the *boppli* is all ready and waiting."

Hannah and Anita had given Sam's old crib a fresh coat of white paint, and Hannah was nearly finished making the quilt. They'd pushed the double bed over to one side of the bedroom, and there was more than enough room for the crib in Anita's large bedroom.

"I think it'll be a boy," Hannah said.

"It doesn't matter to me."

"Have a lie down, Anita, and then you'll be fresh for Simon's visit."

Anita frowned and looked across the kitchen at Hannah. *"Nee,* I have to help you."

"Off you go." Hannah made shooing motions with both hands. "Both boys are sleeping, so I can get plenty done before they wake up."

"I'll just have a little sleep, then. If that's all right?"

"*Jah.* I want you to be well rested."

Anita walked into her bedroom wondering if Hannah guessed that she was starting to feel fond of Simon. She lay down on her bed; a rest was just what she needed.

When Anita woke, she wasn't sure she hadn't slept the whole night and missed dinner. She walked to the bathroom and splashed cold water on her face, and then headed out to the kitchen.

She opened the door and immediately smelled the roasted chicken and vegetables. Then she heard men's voices in the living room.

"There you are. I was just about to go and wake you," Hannah said.

"Simon's already here?"

"*Jah.* He's in the living room."

Anita looked over at the boys' empty table. "Where are the boys?"

"They're playing out in the living room. Can you tell everyone to come in now? Dinner's ready."

Anita looked at the set table. "You should've woken me sooner."

"Nee."

Anita was nervous about seeing Simon. She told herself not to be silly, and walked into the living room. Simon and Amos rose to their feet when she entered the room.

"Dinner ready?" Amos asked.

"Hello, Anita," Simon said.

"Hello, Simon, and *jah,* dinner is ready."

"Come on, Ben, Sam," Amos called to the boys.

The boys left their wooden toys at the side of the room, and followed them into the kitchen. Anita put the boys' food in front of them, and then sat down at the table.

After the silent prayers were said, Amos rubbed his hands together. "This looks *gut.*"

Simon nodded. "It does, Hannah." He looked at Anita. "And, Anita."

"I'm afraid I was asleep, and left Hannah to cook the dinner all on her own."

"You're not sick, are you?" Simon asked.

Amos said, "The midwife was here to see her, and everything's fine."

Anita nodded.

"I'm happy to hear it. You should come and look at my newly painted rooms."

"You've done it already?" Anita asked.

"I have. And you made a *wunderbaar* choice of color." He looked at Hannah and said, "Why don't you and Anita walk the boys over tomorrow?"

"After the meeting?" Hannah asked.

"I forgot the meeting was on tomorrow. *Jah,* come after the meeting."

Hannah smiled. "We'd like that. We don't visit often enough."

The dinner went without a cross word or

argument. Both Hannah and Amos took the boys upstairs to put them to bed.

"Amos seems to have a different attitude toward me now," Simon said.

"I know he does."

"Have you said anything to him?"

"I've said a lot to him, but I've got no idea what made the difference. Maybe Hannah said something."

They had a few more minutes alone before Hannah and Amos came back down the stairs.

THE NEXT DAY'S gathering was held at Hans Yoder's *haus*. Anita and Hannah had just reached the back row, when Anita felt strong pains.

"I think the *boppli's* coming," she whispered to Hannah.

"What? Now?"

"Jah, I had pains all night, but they were mild so I thought they were nothing. Only now they're getting worse."

"Anita, you should've said something sooner. I'll tell Amos, and then Dora can follow us."

Anita looked over at Dora, who was looking at them and seemed to sense what was going on. When Hannah took the two boys to tell Amos what was happening, Dora hurried over to Anita.

"Is it time?" Anita asked.

"Jah," Dora said. "I think it is. I'll drive you to Amos' house."

Just as they walked out of the house, Simon came running after her. "Anita, are you all right?"

Dora held up her hand in front of his face. "It's her time. It's a time when she needs women around her, not men."

Simon nodded and stepped back. Anita gave him a little smile before Dora had her walking to the buggy.

Six hours later, Daniel Joshua Graber was born. Anita held the tiny bundle in her arms and looked down at him. Dora had wrapped him in a white cotton wrap, with nothing showing except his tiny dark-pink hands and his face. Hannah had stayed beside her the whole time.

"He's so beautiful, Anita," Hannah said. "I can't wait for Ben and Sam to get back from *mamm's haus* so they can see him."

"He's a miracle. I can't keep my eyes from him."

The midwife was now busy cleaning up the room. "He's a fine *bu.*"

"I'll tell Amos he's born," Hannah said.

"He would've heard him cry," Dora said bluntly.

Hannah ignored Dora and left the room.

When Hannah came back into the room a moment later, she sat next to Anita. "Amos is excited, and so is Simon."

"Simon's here?"

"He's been here the whole time, waiting with Amos. They'd like to see both of you."

"Let me clean up first," Dora said. "There are some things men were never meant to see."

Hannah and Anita smiled at each other.

Hannah sighed. "Daniel makes me long for another *boppli*."

"I'm certain you'll have more," Anita said. "Many more."

"Was the birth what you'd thought it would be?" Hannah asked.

"I guess it wasn't too far different than what people had told me. It wasn't as bad as some of them had said."

Dora opened the door that led outside to take a load of things to her buggy. When she came back, she said, "All done. You can let the men in now, if you must."

Hannah opened the door, and called Amos and Simon in. Simon let Amos go ahead of him to get his first look at his nephew.

"I can't let anyone have a hold of him because I can't let go of him just yet," Anita joked.

Amos moved away, and let Simon come forward to see Daniel.

"He's lovely, Anita," Simon said.

Anita stared down at the bundle in her arms. "Yes he is."

"Now is he my nephew once removed, or is it by marriage?" he spoke in a high voice.

Anita laughed at him mimicking Fran. "He's your nephew, and I don't know about the rest. It's too much for me to think about right now."

CHAPTER 18

This book of the law shall not depart out of thy mouth; but thou shalt meditate therein day and night, that thou mayest observe to do according to all that is written therein: for then thou shalt make thy way prosperous, and then thou shalt have good success.
Joshua 1:8

*O*ver the next year, life for Anita and Daniel settled into a routine. Simon had gone back to his pattern of having dinner a few times a week at Hannah and Amos' house. He was often included when the family group attended community events, and he and Anita continued to enjoy each other's company.

It was after one of those family dinners that Simon had an opportunity to have a private word with Anita.

"On Tuesday, after Hannah goes to work, Amos will be out working on the farm." He laughed. "I've rehearsed this, and now I can't remember what I'm supposed to say."

Anita smiled. "Just say it plainly."

"I want you to come somewhere with me; you and Daniel."

"Aren't you supposed to be working, telling your men what to do?"

"I'm the boss. They can do without me for one day. I want to take Daniel on his first outing."

"He's been on lots of outings."

"Not with me. I'll take him on his first buggy ride in *my* buggy."

Anita giggled, and nodded. "I'll look forward to it."

They were interrupted when Amos came back into the room.

"What were you two talking about?"

Anita and Simon looked at each other, and Amos raised his hands. "Don't tell me." Amos sat down shaking his head.

Simon left not long after that, and Anita went into her room. She stared at her sleeping baby. Anita was excited about seeing Simon the next day and wanted to share it with someone, but there was no one to tell.

She leaned over and whispered to Daniel,

who had just moved into his big boy's bed, "I'll never let you forget your *Dat.* Joshua is your *vadder,* and when you get bigger, I've got so many stories I can tell you about him."

She leaned down close to his face and kissed him gently on his soft cheek before changing into her nightgown and getting into her own bed.

THE NEXT DAY, they were with Simon in his buggy. "And where are we going? Can you tell me yet?"

"I'm going to take you both on a picnic."

"Daniel and I love picnics."

Simon stopped the buggy between his place and Amos' house. He led them to the place where they'd run into each other not long after she'd arrived. She'd been making daisy chains and he'd been checking on his fences.

He had a blanket spread out already and a large picnic basket was on one side. There were limp daisy chains on the blanket. He picked one up, and laughed. "They didn't look like this when I made them yesterday."

"You made them yesterday, and they've had no water?" Anita laughed at him. "It was so nice of you to do this for us." She looked down at Daniel who had recently had his first birthday. "Say 'denke, Onkel Simon.'"

Daniel waved his arms and jabbered a few sounds in response, trying to decide if he liked crawling on the ground.

"I didn't do it for Daniel. Although it was nice of him to join us." He stared into her eyes. "I did it for you. Let's sit."

Anita was pleased. She smiled at him when they'd sat down, and then she looked away.

"Do you think that Amos is right about our age difference?" Simon asked.

"*Jah*, you're far too old for me. I need to look for someone younger."

"I'm serious, Anita."

Anita gulped as she looked into his eyes. The joking was over. He was being serious, and she knew she had to give a straightforward answer. "I think age doesn't matter. It might matter if it were a large age gap or if the younger person was still a teenager, but a slight difference shouldn't be a problem."

"Do you remember the list that Fran gave you a long time ago?"

"*Jah.* I don't think I'll ever forget Fran's list."

He pulled the paper out of his pocket.

She stared at the paper. "You kept it?"

He nodded.

"I wondered where it got to."

He held the paper in one hand, and with the other hand reached into the basket and pulled out a pin. "I need to ask you an important question, Anita Graber."

Anita's heart pounded. Was he going to ask her to marry him? She realized she wanted him to.

When he hesitated, she asked, "What question?"

He smiled. "I've added my name to Fran's list."

Anita put her hand to her mouth and giggled.

"I was hoping that you might take this piece of paper and this pin, and if you happen to stick the pin in my name, I'm hoping you'll agree to marry me."

"And what if the pin sticks in someone else's name?"

"You won't have to marry him. We won't let him know about it, but if you do stick the pin in my name, you'll have to marry me. What do you say?"

"This is a big decision. And we're leaving it up to chance?"

"We're leaving it up to *Gott*. This is how

239

the bishops are chosen. Well, not with a pin, but by lot, which is a similar principle."

"Are you prepared for the outcome?" Anita's heart pounded hard against her chest.

"More than prepared. I've been thinking for a long time about asking you to marry me, but at the same time giving you a way out."

Anita stretched out her hand. "Give me the paper."

"You have to close your eyes, and I'll put the pin and the paper in your hands when you tell me you're ready."

"Since when do you make all the rules?"

"Shh. This is my idea, so I make the rules. Now close your eyes and tell me when you're ready."

"Okay, but you have to keep an eye on Daniel. He's been trying to walk, and I don't want to miss his first steps." She glanced down at Daniel who was sitting next to her, playing happily with the limp daisy chains.

Then she closed her eyes and silently prayed that *Gott* would help her choose his name if he were the man for her. And she hoped that he was. She left it in *Gott's* hands, and without opening her eyes, said, "I'm ready."

She placed her hands out and Simon carefully placed the pin between the thumb and forefinger of her right hand, and then placed the paper in her other hand.

"Now I've unfolded the paper, and it's the right side up. You've got no idea where I could've put my name. I don't want you to think I've put it at the bottom."

"Which is the top and which is the bottom?"

"I've handed it to you with the top at the top, and the bottom at the bottom."

"And what happens if I don't stick the pin in your name?"

"Everything in life can't be planned, Anita. Sometimes you have to take chances."

With her eyes still closed, she nodded.

She placed the paper down in front of her on the blanket, circled the pin and then pushed the pin into the paper. When he remained silent, she was certain that she's missed his name. "Can I open my eyes now?"

"*Jah.*"

Anita opened her eyes and looked down at the list. She saw that it wasn't Fran's list at all, and what's more, every spot on the page held Simon's name. She looked up at him and laughed. "I knew it."

"*Nee* you didn't."

"*Jah,* I thought you might have done something like that."

He leaned over. "Will you marry me, Anita Graber?"

She nodded. "I will."

He leaned over and gently pressed his lips against hers.

"I have to marry you now. I said I would if the pin stuck you."

"You're exactly right."

They both laughed, and Daniel clapped his hands and joined in.

"When do you think we should tell Amos and Hannah?" Anita asked, wondering what their reactions would be.

"A year or two."

"That's most likely for the best," Anita said. "But who knows what man Fran will try and make me marry before then."

"Perhaps we should marry as soon as we can?"

Anita nodded. "Perhaps."

"I do have that list, you know - Fran's list - the real one. I kept it as a reminder."

Anita laughed. "A reminder of what?"

"A reminder that I shouldn't let you out of my sight for too long." He smiled at her. "You're the only woman I've ever been able to talk to."

Anita's face hurt from smiling so much. "Really?"

"*Jah.* I knew there was something about

you from the moment I first saw you walk into the kitchen at Amos and Hannah's house."

"I felt a certain fondness toward you too, back then, but it seemed no one else thought we'd make a match."

He took hold of her hand. "It never matters what others think. We're the ones who have to live our lives. As long as we're not hurting other people, it shouldn't matter who we love."

"It doesn't matter. You can remember to say all that when we go back to the *haus* to tell Amos."

Simon cleared his throat. "I'll let you do the talking."

"The one who does the asking is the one who has to do the talking. You asked me to marry you, so you have to tell Amos."

He pulled a sad face. "Okay." He leaned down and kissed Daniel on top of his head.

"I'll hold Daniel in my arms while I tell him, so Amos can't hit me."

"That's not a bad idea." Anita thought back to the old man on the bus who'd given her words of comfort over a year ago. As he'd promised, time had made things easier. She no longer dwelt on trying to figure out why Joshua was taken from her. For Daniel, she had to live in the present and be happy. God had given her Simon now, a wonderful man to be happy with, and God had blessed her with a son. How could she be sad any longer?

After they enjoyed some private time together, Anita and Simon, and Daniel went back that evening to tell Hannah and Amos their news.

Truly my soul waiteth upon God: from him cometh my salvation. He only is my rock and my salvation; he is my defence; I shall not be greatly moved.

Psalm 62:1

Thank you for reading Amish Widow's Hope.

www.SamanthaPriceAuthor.com

THE NEXT BOOK IN THE SERIES

Book 2
The Pregnant Amish Widow

When Grace's abusive husband died, she couldn't wait to return to her Amish community. Soon, Grace found out her old crush was still single. She had high hopes for marriage with someone who wasn't going to terrorise her as her late husband had. But with younger women vying for her his attention, would he give a pregnant widow a second thought?

ALL SAMANTHA PRICE'S SERIES

Amish Maids Trilogy
A 3 book Amish romance series of novels featuring 5 friends finding love.

Amish Love Blooms
A 6 book Amish romance series of novels about four sisters and their cousins.

Amish Misfits
A series of 7 stand-alone books about people who have never fitted in.

The Amish Bonnet Sisters
To date there are 28 books in this continuing family saga. My most popular and best-selling series.

Amish Women of Pleasant Valley
An 8 book Amish romance series with the same characters. This has been one of my most popular series.

Ettie Smith Amish Mysteries
An ongoing cozy mystery series with octo-genarian sleuths. Popular with lovers of mysteries such as Miss Marple or Murder She Wrote.

Amish Secret Widows' Society
A ten novella mystery/romance series - a prequel to the Ettie Smith Amish Mysteries.

Expectant Amish Widows

A stand-alone Amish romance series of 19 books.

Seven Amish Bachelors
A 7 book Amish Romance series following the Fuller brothers' journey to finding love.

Amish Foster Girls
A 4 book Amish romance series with the same characters who have been fostered to an Amish family.

Amish Brides
An Amish historical romance. 5 book series with the same characters who have arrived in America to start their new life.

Amish Romance Secrets
The first series I ever wrote. 6 novellas following the same characters.

Amish Christmas Books

Each year I write an Amish Christmas stand-alone romance novel.

Amish Twin Hearts
A 4 book Amish Romance featuring twins and their friends.

Amish Wedding Season
The second series I wrote. It has the same characters throughout the 5 books.

Gretel Koch Jewel Thief
A clean 5 book suspense/mystery series about a jewel thief who has agreed to consult with the FBI.